This book belongs to

People's most intimate memories are tied up with gifts they have lovingly given and received.

Inspirations Gifts is a collection of fabulous projects, each ideally suited for someone you love.

All projects come with full instructions for every stitch and technique used, making this publication a wonderful gift in itself.

Please enjoy the superb embroidery ideas, glorious photographs and comprehensive instructions in the following pages.

Susan O'Connor
Editor

INSPIRATIONS GIFTS

THIS PUBLICATION IS DEDICATED TO THE
WORLD'S MOST BEAUTIFUL READERS

PROUDLY PRODUCED AND PRINTED IN AUSTRALIA.

COUNTRY BUMPKIN PUBLICATIONS

Box 194, Kent Town

South Australia 5071

76A Kensington Road, Rose Park

South Australia 5067

Ph (08) 8364 1075

Fax (08) 8364 0479

Email: cbumpkin@ozemail.com.au

CONTENTS
INSPIRATIONS GIFTS

STITCH INDEX

HINTS

TECHNIQUES

CENTRE LIFTOUT PATTERNS

The French Connection ~ Simple Pleasures ~ The Maiden's Blush ~ Journey's End

Dolce Vita ~ Rambling Rose ~ Treasures

VANITY FAIR

Beautifully embroidered linen handkerchiefs

DESIGNED BY KRIS RICHARDS OF SOUTH AUSTRALIA

A blue-violet ribbon embraces a gentle posy of pink roses and cream daisies on a purchased linen handkerchief with a pinstitched edge.

REQUIREMENTS

1 x 26cm square (10 ¼") white linen handkerchief with pinstitched edge

Threads & Needles

DMC stranded cotton

A = 224 vy lt shell pink

B = 647 med beaver grey

C = 746 off-white

D = 819 lt baby pink

E = 3024 vy lt brown-grey

F = 3743 vy lt antique violet

Madeira stranded silk

G = 0901 lt blue-violet

No. 9 straw (milliner's) needle

No. 10 crewel needle

Supplies

10cm wide (4") embroidery hoop

Sharp lead pencil

EMBROIDERY PREPARATION

See the centre liftout for the embroidery design.

With the right side facing you, place the handkerchief over the design in the centre liftout, matching the placement marks below the design with the corner of the handkerchief. Pin in place to prevent movement. Trace the design onto the corner using the pencil.

THIS DESIGN USES:

Split stitch   Satin stitch
Detached chain   Bullion knot
French knot   Stem stitch
Padded satin stitch

EMBROIDERY

Place the fabric in the hoop to work the satin stitch bow, taking care not to distort the grain of the fabric. Remove the fabric from the hoop for all other embroidery.

After finishing the bow, stitch the six pale pink roses. To form the padded satin stitch centre for each rose, work a square of four horizontal satin stitches and overlay these with four vertical satin stitches. Add three bullion knots for the petals of the smaller roses and four bullion knots for the petals of the larger roses.

Stitch the rosebuds with bullion knots and the cream daisies with detached chain petals and french knot centres.

Embroider the pale green leaves near the daisies and rosebuds.

The stems and leaves of the sprigs are worked next, followed by the pale pink french knot buds.

Within the posy, work clusters of three french knots with the darker pink thread and scattered knots with the antique violet thread.

Use the straw needle for all bullion knots and the crewel needle for all other embroidery.

EMBROIDERY KEY

All embroidery is worked using two strands of thread unless otherwise specified.

Bow

Outlines = G (1 strand, split stitch)
Loops and ties = G (1 strand, satin stitch)
Bow knot = G (1 strand, padded satin stitch)

Roses

Centre = D (padded satin stitch)
Petals = D (3 - 4 bullion knots, 10 wraps)

Rosebuds

Petals = D (2 bullion knots, 7 wraps or 1 bullion knot, 6 wraps)
Leaves = E (1 strand, detached chain)

Daisies

Centre = C (french knot, 1 wrap)
Petals = C (detached chain)
Leaves = E (1 strand, detached chain)

Sprigs

Buds = D (french knot, 1 wrap)
Stems = B (1 strand, stem stitch)
Leaves = B (1 strand, detached chain)

French knots

Clusters = A (3 french knots, 2 wraps)
Scattered knots = F (french knot, 1 - 2 wraps)

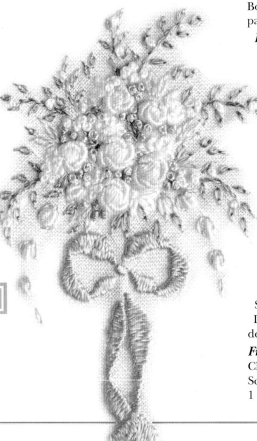

SATIN STITCH BOW WITH SPLIT STITCH OUTLINE

Split stitch is used to outline the bow. It gives a smoother, more stable edge than running stitch.

It is important to angle the needle under the split stitch when coming to the front and going to the back.

The bow knot is padded satin stitch.

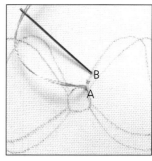

1. Secure the thread with a tiny back stitch on the back of the fabric. **Split stitch.** Bring the thread up at A. Take a small stitch from A to B.

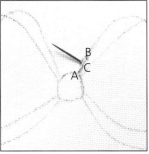

2. Bring the needle to the front at C, halfway between A and B, splitting the thread of the previous stitch.

3. Work split stitch along one traced line and then work along the second traced line to complete the loop outline.

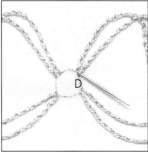

4. Work the outline of the left bow loop in the same manner. **Satin stitch.** Bring needle to front at D, just outside split stitch outline.

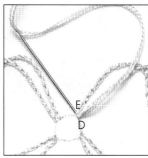

5. Take the needle to the back at E over the split stitch outline, opposite D. Angle the needle under the split stitch before taking it to the back.

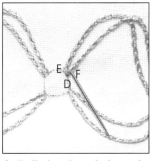

6. Pull the thread through, keeping an even tension. **Completed first satin stitch.** Bring the needle to the front at F, as close as possible to D.

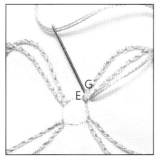

7. Take the needle to the back at G, as close as possible to E.

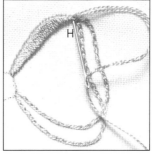

8. Continue stitching to the first ribbon twist keeping stitches parallel. Complete the last stitch before twist by taking needle to back at H.

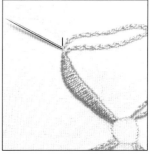

9. Rotate the fabric. Bring the needle to the front at I.

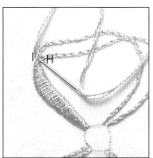

10. Take the needle to the back at H.

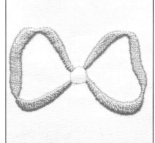

11. Continue stitching as before, rotating the fabric at each twist. Complete the second bow loop in the same manner.

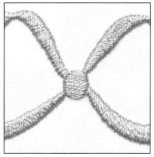

12. Bow knot. The bow knot is padded satin stitch. Work horizontal satin stitches across the bow knot.

13. Work a layer of vertical satin stitches over the first layer to complete the bow knot. The ties are stitched in the same manner as the loops.

A delicate shadow-worked heart filled with a pale mauve lattice is decorated with glorious bullion roses and buds.

REQUIREMENTS

1 x 26cm square (10 ¼") white linen handkerchief with pinstitched edge

Threads & Needles

DMC stranded cotton
A = 712 cream
B = 819 lt baby pink
C = 3012 med khaki green
D = 3713 vy lt salmon
E = 3733 dusky rose
F = 3743 vy lt antique violet
No. 9 straw (milliner's) needle
No. 10 crewel needle

Supplies

10cm wide (4") embroidery hoop
Sharp lead pencil

EMBROIDERY PREPARATION

See the centre liftout for the embroidery design.

With the right side facing you, place the handkerchief over the design in the centre liftout, matching the placement marks below the design with the corner of the handkerchief. Pin in place to prevent movement. Trace the design onto the corner using the lead pencil.

EMBROIDERY

Place the handkerchief into the hoop, taking care not to distort the grain of the fabric. Embroider the six segments of shadow work for the heart outline. Remove the fabric from the hoop to complete the remainder of the design.

Stitch the lines of stem stitch within the heart, working all the lines in one direction before stitching those in the other direction.

The bullion roses are embroidered next, starting each one from its centre and working outwards.

Work the bullion rosebuds, followed by the detached chain leaves. The cream and violet french knot buds are stitched last.

Use the straw needle for all bullion knots and the crewel needle for all other embroidery.

THIS DESIGN USES:

*Shadow work   Bullion knot
Stem stitch   French knot
Detached chain*

STEP-BY-STEP STITCH INSTRUCTIONS NOT INCLUDED IN THIS ARTICLE CAN BE FOUND ON THE FOLLOWING PAGES.

Bullion knot - page 59
Detached chain - page 46
French knot - page 40
Stem stitch - page 46

EMBROIDERY KEY

All embroidery is worked using two strands of thread unless otherwise specified.

Heart

Outline = F (1 strand, shadow work)
Lattice = F (1 strand, stem stitch)

Large side-view roses

Centre = E (1 bullion knot, 4 wraps)
Inner petals = D (3 bullion knots, 7 wraps)
Outer petals = B (5 bullion knots, 7 wraps)

Large full rose

Centre = E (1 bullion knot, 4 wraps)
Inner petals = D (2 bullion knots, 6 wraps)
Outer petals = B (6 bullion knots, 7 wraps)

Small roses

Centre = E (1 bullion knot, 4 wraps)
Outer petals = D (3 bullion knots, 4 wraps)

Rosebuds = B (1 - 2 bullion knots, 4 wraps)

Tiny buds = A or F (french knot, 1 - 2 wraps)

Leaves = C (1 strand, detached chain)

SHADOW WORK

The delicate effect of shading is created by the colour of the embroidery thread showing through from the wrong side of fine fabrics.

The stitch can be worked from either the right or wrong side of the fabric. Here it is worked from the right side and is known as double back stitch.

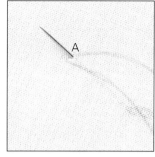

1. Begin with a waste knot. Bring the needle to the front at A on the upper line, 1.5mm (1/16") away from the point of the shape.

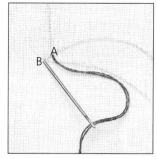

2. Pull the thread through. Take the needle to the back at B, exactly on the point.

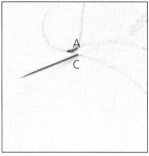

3. Pull the thread through. Re-emerge at C, on the lower line directly below A.

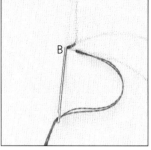

4. Pull the thread through. Take the needle to the back at B using the same hole in the fabric as before.

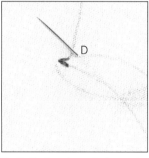

5. Pull the thread through. Re-emerge at D on the upper line, 1.5mm (1/16") away from A.

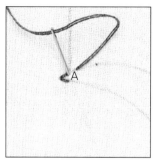

6. Pull the thread through. Take the needle to the back at A, using exactly the same hole in the fabric as before.

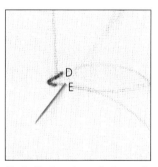

7. Pull the thread through and re-emerge at E on the lower line (opposite D).

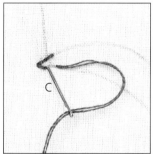

8. Pull the thread through. Take the needle to the back at C, using the same hole in the fabric.

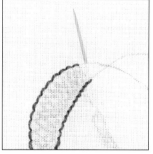

9. Continue working stitches in the same manner as steps 5 to 8. To work a curve, the stitches on the inside line are gradually reduced in length.

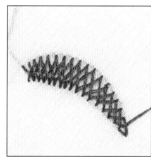

10. Photograph showing the wrong side of the fabric where the stitches form *closed herringbone stitch.*

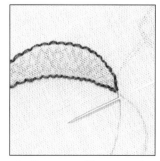

11. Crossover. To create the effect of twisting, the lower curve crosses over the upper curve. Work the first stitch of the crossover on lower line.

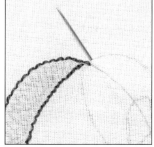

12. Pull the thread through. Bring the needle to the front on the upper line for the second stitch of the crossover.

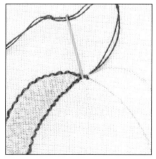

13. Take it to the back to the left of the intersection on the lower line.

14. Continue stitching as before. To end off or begin a new thread, weave through the threads on the wrong side, close to the edge.

THE FRENCH CONNECTION

A magnificent ivory
silk coathanger
designed by
Denise Bakes
of Tasmania

Pairs of twin-needle tucks form the subtle background for the wound ribbon roses. A bow, fashioned from two shades of pink ribbon, decorates the satin-covered hook.

REQUIREMENTS

Fabric
30cm x 50cm wide (12" x 20") piece of ivory silk dupion

Ribbons, Threads & Needles
YLI silk ribbon 4mm wide ($^3/_{16}$")
A = 50cm (20") no. 128 deep musk
B = 80cm (31 $^1/_2$") no. 68 fuchsia pink
C = 1.5m (59") no. 7 blush
Madeira stranded silk
D = 0813 lt shell pink
E = 1309 pistachio green
No. 26 tapestry needle
No. 9 crewel needle

Supplies
38cm long (15") wooden coathanger
25cm x 183cm wide (10" x 72") thick polyester wadding
1.3m x 20mm wide (51" x $^3/_4$") ivory satin bias binding
110cm (43") size 00 piping cord
Water-soluble fabric marker

EMBROIDERY PREPARATION

See the centre liftout for the full-size pattern and embroidery designs.

Pintucks
The piece of silk fabric is pintucked before transferring the pattern and design markings.

Using the fabric marker and with the right side of the fabric facing you, rule diagonal lines at 4cm (1 $^5/_8$") intervals across the entire piece of fabric *(see diag 1)*. Rule a second set of lines at 4cm(1 $^5/_8$") intervals in the opposite direction *(diag1)*.

Diag 1

Using matching thread and a twin needle, stitch pintucks along the first set of ruled lines. On the left side of each tuck, stitch a parallel tuck approximately 4mm ($^3/_{16}$") away.

Stitch pintucks along the second set of ruled lines. On the left side of each tuck, stitch a parallel tuck in the same manner as before.

Rinse the pintucked fabric in cold water to remove all traces of the fabric marker. Allow the fabric to dry. Place on a soft well-padded surface and press on the wrong side.

Transferring the designs

With right side facing, place the fabric over the pattern in the centre liftout, aligning the pintucks with the lines on the pattern.

Using the fabric marker, trace the embroidery designs and all pattern markings.

Reposition the fabric over the pattern piece for the back of the coathanger cover. Mark the cutting lines with the fabric marker.

It is not necessary to align the pintucks with the lines on the fabric but do ensure the pintucks are centred across the pattern area.

Complete the embroidery before cutting out the front and back pieces along the marked cutting lines.

EMBROIDERY

Nine pink roses and buds are sprinkled across a trellis of pintucks on this delightful coathanger cover.

Stitch the roses first, using three shades of pink ribbon. Work a ribbon stitch bud adjacent to each rose.

Add a fly stitch calyx around each bud and then a straight stitch stem and single detached chain leaf below each calyx.

To finish, embroider three pairs of detached chain leaves around each full-blown rose.

Use the crewel needle for all thread embroidery and the tapestry needle for all ribbon embroidery.

EMBROIDERY KEY

All thread embroidery is worked using two strands unless otherwise specified.

Roses
Framework = D (1 strand, 5 straight stitches)
Centre = A (wound ribbon rose)
Inner petals = B (wound ribbon rose)
Outer petals = C (wound ribbon rose)
Leaves = E (detached chain)

Buds
Petal = C (ribbon stitch)
Calyx = E (fly stitch)
Stem = E (straight stitch)
Leaf = E (detached chain)

CONSTRUCTION

See page 66 for step-by-step instructions to assemble the coathanger.

STEP-BY-STEP STITCH INSTRUCTIONS NOT INCLUDED IN THIS ARTICLE CAN BE FOUND ON THE FOLLOWING PAGES.

Detached chain - page 46
Straight stitch - page 28

THIS DESIGN USES:

*Detached chain   Straight stitch
Fly stitch   Ribbon stitch
Wound ribbon rose*

RIBBON STITCH

This stitch is worked in ribbon only.
It is worked as a straight stitch with a tightened loop at one end to anchor the ribbon.
Leaves, short stems and flower petals are often worked in ribbon stitch.

  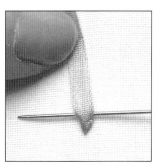 

1. Bring the ribbon to the front at the base of the stitch.

2. Lay the ribbon flat on the fabric. Hold in place with the left thumb just beyond the required length of the stitch.

3. Place the needle under the ribbon at the base.

4. Using a slight upward pressure, move the needle towards the thumb to spread the ribbon.

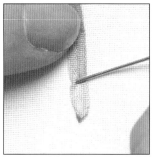   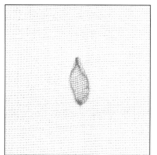

5. Place the point of the needle on the centre of the ribbon at the position for the tip of the stitch.

6. Take the needle through the ribbon and fabric to the back of the work.

7. Place your thumb over the stitch to keep it flat and untwisted on the fabric. Pull the ribbon through gently.

8. Pull until the ribbon begins to curl along the sides. **Completed ribbon stitch.**

FLY STITCH

Fly stitch is an open detached chain stitch with many variations. It is worked from left to right and in the shape of a V or a Y depending on the length of the anchoring stitch.

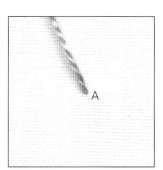 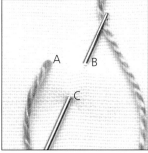 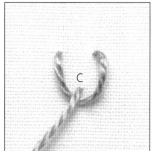 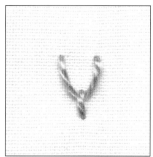

1. Bring the thread to the front at A. This will be the left hand side of the stitch.

2. Take the needle to the back at B and re-emerge at C. Loop the thread under the tip of the needle and to the right.

3. Hold the looped thread in place with the left thumb. Pull the needle through until the looped thread lies snugly against C.

4. Take the thread to the back a short distance below C to anchor the fly stitch. **Completed fly stitch.**

WOUND RIBBON ROSE

This easy-to-stitch, textured rose is created by weaving ribbon through a framework of straight stitch spokes.

The spokes are worked first, using embroidery thread, with each one being based on the hour positions of a clock face. Use an odd number of spokes.

To begin and end off the ribbon, catch it to the stitching on the back of the work with sewing thread.

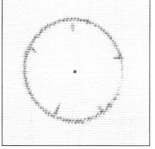

1. Framework. Draw a circle and mark the centre. Imagining the circle is a clock face, mark the outer edge at 12, 2, 5, 7 and 10 o'clock.

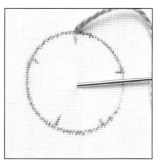

2. Using thread, bring the needle to the front at the 12 o'clock mark. Take it to the back at the centre.

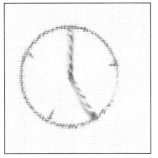

3. Pull through to form a straight stitch. Re-emerge at the 5 o'clock mark and take to the back at the centre to form the second stitch.

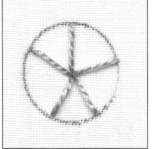

4. Work a stitch from the 7 o'clock mark to the centre. Work stitches from 10 o'clock and 2 o'clock in the same manner.

5. Petals. Bring the darkest shade of ribbon to the front between two spokes as close as possible to the centre.

6. Working in an anti-clockwise direction, weave the ribbon over and under the spokes of the framework until one round is complete.

7. Pull this round firmly so the threads of the framework do not show through the centre.

8. Weave a second round, allowing the ribbon to twist and loosening the tension slightly.

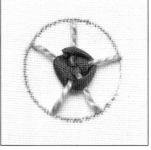

9. Take needle to back between two spokes, after weaving over a spoke. Pull ribbon through. Cut off excess leaving a 1cm (3/8") tail.

10. Using the medium shade of ribbon, emerge next to where the darkest ribbon went to the back.

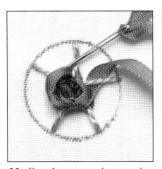

11. Continue weaving, maintaining the over and under sequence for two more rounds. Take the ribbon to the back in the same manner as before.

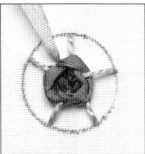

12. Bring the lightest shade of ribbon to the front between the spokes just next to where the last ribbon was taken to the back.

13. Continue weaving until the framework is entirely hidden. Take the needle over one more spoke. Tuck it under the next spoke to take to the back.

14. Pull the ribbon through. On the wrong side, cut the ribbon. Secure any uncaught tails of ribbon with thread. **Completed wound ribbon rose.**

CONSTRUCTING THE COATHANGER

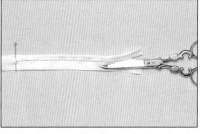

The cover is finished with ivory satin piping and the hook is enclosed by satin bias rouleau.

The wooden coathanger is padded with strips of wadding.

After the embroidery is complete, cut out the front and back along the marked cutting lines.

Our coathanger is a sample only.

1. Hook cover. Cut 28cm (11") of satin bias binding. Press flat. With right sides together, fold in half lengthwise. Mark the centre with a pin.

Starting at one end and using a tiny zigzag, stitch 6mm (1/4") from fold. Stitch to the centre mark. Trim seam allowance close to the stitching.

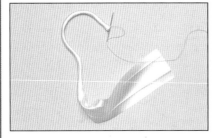

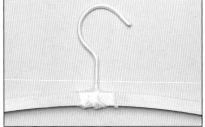

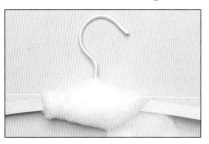

2. Turn through with a loop turner. Slip the cover over the hook. Turn under the raw end at the tip of the hook. Using a fine needle and matching thread, slipstitch the opening closed.

3. Ensure the cover is firm and smooth over the hook. Wrap the tail of the bias strip around the coathanger, and secure with small stitches.

4. Padding. Cut the wadding into 7.5cm wide (3") strips. Starting from the hook, wrap the first piece very firmly around the coat hanger.

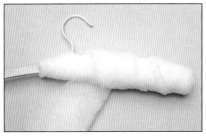

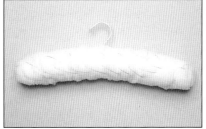

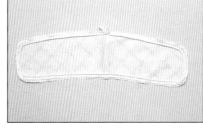

5. When nearing the end of the coathanger, fold a piece of wadding over the end and continue wrapping the strip over it.

6. Wrap the remaining side in the same manner. Continue wrapping across both sides until the entire coathanger is well padded. Join in new pieces of wadding at different places to avoid lumps. Secure the wadding with large tacking stitches.

7. Make the piping from the cord and remaining satin bias binding. Pin the piping to the right side of the front. Start and finish at the mark for the hook. Overlap the end of the piping over the start, curving the raw ends into the seam allowance. Clip heading to ease around the curves.

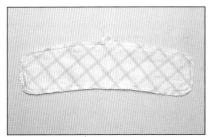

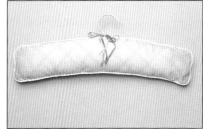

8. With right sides together and raw edges even, pin and stitch the front and back together between the marked points, following the previous row of stitching.

9. Turn the cover to the right side and place over the padded hanger. Fold under the seam allowances along the lower edge. Slipstitch the opening closed.

10. Cut two pieces of ribbon (B and C), each 36cm (14") long. Place the two pieces together and tie in a bow at the base of the hook.
Completed coathanger.

LES PETITES FLEURES

DESIGNED BY SHARON PATON OF VICTORIA

THE GIFT OF A LIFETIME

LES PETITES FLEURES

THE LITTLE FLOWERS

A GORGEOUS COMBINATION
OF STRIPED SILK WITH AN ELEGANT FINALE OF RIBBON
ROSES TIED WITH A SKY BLUE BOW.

LIKE A PERFECT MEMORY IT WILL LAST FOREVER.

Seven lemon folded ribbon roses are tightly clustered
together and held by an organza bow. Dainty in its dimensions,
the cushion is finished with piping, a ruched frill and opulent striped cord.
Green ribbon french knots are worked between the roses.

REQUIREMENTS

Fabric

45cm x 112cm wide (17 3/4" x 44")
striped silk dupion

Thread, Ribbons & Needles

Anchor stranded cotton
A = 846 dk avocado green
YLI pure silk ribbon
4mm wide (3/16")
B = 2m (2yd 7") no. 21
hunter green
Double-sided satin ribbon
10mm wide (3/8")
C = 2m (2yd 7") lemon
Mokuba no. 4546 crepe georgette
ribbon 15mm wide (5/8")
D = 25cm (10") no. 21 sky blue
No. 22 chenille needle
No. 8 crewel needle
No. 10 crewel needle

Supplies

93cm x 1cm wide (36 1/2" x 3/8")
piping cord
1m (40") size 00 piping cord
1m (40") blue and gold
twisted cord
15cm (6") lemon zip
21cm x 50cm wide (8 1/4" x 19 5/8")
very fine interlining for insert
80g (3oz) polyester fibre-fill
for insert
Sharp lead pencil

CUTTING OUT

See the centre liftout for the
cutting layout.

Cut a rectangle 20cm x 23cm wide
(7 7/8" x 9") from the striped silk
fabric for the cushion front.
Ensure that the centre stripe is a
blue stripe.

Cut a second rectangle 21cm x
23cm wide (8 1/4" x 9") for the
cushion back. For the ruched
frill, cut four pieces each 70cm x
10cm wide (27 1/2" x 4").

Cut two strips 45cm x 3cm wide
(17 3/4" x 1 1/4") for the piping.
Ensure the centre is a blue stripe.

EMBROIDERY PREPARATION

See the centre liftout for the
embroidery design.

Stitch around all sides of the
cushion front with a zigzag or
overlock stitch to prevent the
fabric fraying.

On the right side of the fabric
and with the stripes running
vertically, mark the placement for
the centre rose by measuring
8.5cm (3 3/8") down from the top
edge and 11.5cm (4 1/2") in from
the left hand side edge. This will
be on the centre blue stripe.
Mark the position with the lead
pencil *(diag 1)*.

Diag 1

Trace the embroidery design
onto tracing paper. Matching the
centre rose on the tracing with
the mark on the fabric, pin the
tracing to the fabric.

Using a large needle, pierce holes
in the tracing to mark the positions of the roses, stems and bow.

Make a pencil mark through
each hole in the paper. Remove
the tracing.

EMBROIDERY

An organza ribbon bow gently
ties seven tightly clustered lemon
folded ribbon roses. Silk ribbon
french knots and straight stitch
stems finish the design.

Use the chenille needle for the
ribbon embroidery and the no. 8
crewel needle for the thread
embroidery.

Roses

Cut the lemon satin ribbon into
seven pieces, each 28cm (11")
long. Construct seven folded
ribbon roses following the step-
by-step instructions on page 41.

Securely attach the base of the
centre rose to the fabric using
matching machine sewing thread
and the no. 10 crewel needle. Pin
the remaining six roses so they sit
snug around the centre. Attach in
the same manner as the centre
rose. Stitch the petals together
from the front of the work,
ensuring the stitches are
concealed.

> STEP-BY-STEP
> STITCH INSTRUCTIONS NOT
> INCLUDED IN THIS ARTICLE
> CAN BE FOUND ON THE
> FOLLOWING PAGES.
>
> French knot - page 40
> Straight stitch - page 46

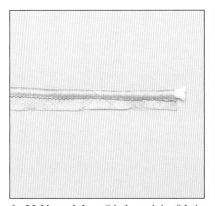

Stems

Work fourteen straight stitches for the stems, varying the length of the stitches and allowing them to overlap. Using two strands of the stranded cotton, work french knots onto the ribbon stems to couch them in place. Tie the crepe georgette ribbon into a bow with loops approximately 2cm (³/₄") long. Using the chenille needle, take the bow ends to the back of the fabric and stitch in place.

Ribbon french knots

Embroider a cluster of 5 - 6 french knots between the roses around the outer edge of the bouquet. Work five french knots around the centre rose. After wrapping the ribbon around the needle, pull through very gently so the knot will sit on the top of the roses and not disappear beneath them.

THIS DESIGN USES:

Folded ribbon rose
French knot
Straight stitch

CONSTRUCTION

To prevent fraying, neaten all raw edges before beginning to assemble the cushion. All seam allowances are 1cm (³/₈") unless otherwise specified.
Ours is a sample only.

1. Making piping. Stitch to join fabric strips. Press seam open. On the wrong side of the fabric strip, place the thin piping cord along the centre. Fold the fabric over the cord, matching raw edges. Stitch close to the cord.

2. Attaching the piping. Start in the middle of the lower side. With right sides together and overlapping the ends, pin piping in place along seamline of cushion front. Clip the heading at the corners. Stitch in place along the stitchline.

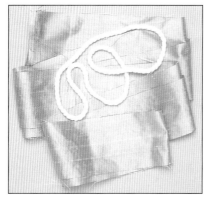

3. Making the ruched frill. Overlap the ends of the thick cord. Stitch together to form a circle. Cover the join with masking tape. With right sides together, join fabric strips to form a circle. Press the seams open. Baste and stitch in place from the right side.

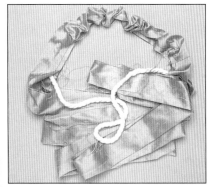

4. With wrong sides together, fold the entire frill in half lengthwise. Place the cord inside the frill. Note: at this stage it will not fit very well. Using long machine stitches, begin to stitch a gathering row around the frill.

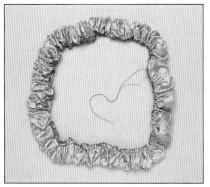

5. Keeping the cord inside, pull up the gathers as you stitch until the frill fits the cord. Do not press.

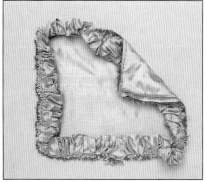

6. Attaching frill. Mark the centre of each side on the cushion front. Matching frill seams with quarter marks, pin the frill to the front. From the wrong side of the cushion front, stitch the frill in place, following the piping stitchline.

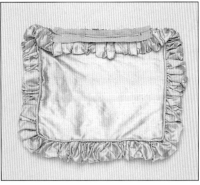

7. Inserting the zip. Zigzag across the top of the zip to hold the tapes together. With right sides facing, centre the zip over the frill on one long side of the cushion front. Tack, baste and machine stitch in place.

8. Neaten and press under the 2cm (3/4") seam allowance along one long side of the back. With right sides together, match this pressed line with the front stitching line. Stitch to the corner at each end, leaving a 15cm (6") opening for the zip.

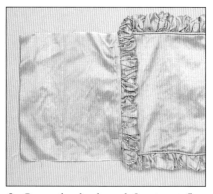

9. Open the back and front out flat. Tack and machine stitch the remaining side of the zip in place from the right side.

10. Completing the back. Open the zip. With right sides together and matching raw edges, pin the back to the front on the remaining unstitched sides. The ruched frill is sandwiched between. Stitch, trim seams and clip corners. Turn to the right side.

11. Making the insert. Fold the interlining in half and cut along the fold. Overlock or zigzag around three sides. Fill the insert with the polyester fibre-fill. Pin the remaining raw edges together and overlock or zigzag.

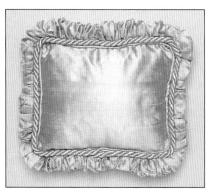

12. Lay the twisted cord just outside the piping. Slipstitch in place. Twist the ends together placing them towards the cushion. Stitch through to secure. Place the insert inside the cushion cover and close the zip. **Completed cushion.**

FOLDED RIBBON ROSE

These decorative roses are made from a length of ribbon.

Different widths and types of ribbon can be used.

The size of the rose is determined by the width of the ribbon and the number of folds.

Each rose is prepared individually and then attached to the fabric using matching sewing thread.

We use contrasting sewing thread for photographic purposes only.

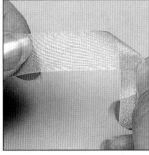

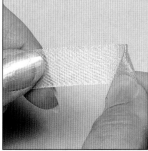

1. Centre. Hold the ribbon horizontally in your left hand. With your right thumb and forefinger, fold the right end over for approximately 2cm ($^3/_4$") at a 90° angle.

2. Holding the ribbon in the left hand and the folded tail in the right hand, roll the ribbon firmly towards the left thumb for one turn.

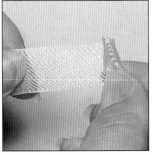

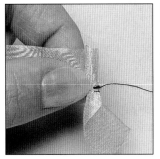

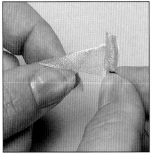

3. Roll twice more to form the centre of the rose.

4. Still holding firmly and using sewing thread, take 2 to 3 tiny stitches through the layers of ribbon. Leave the needle dangling.

5. First petal. With your left thumb and forefinger, fold the top edge of the ribbon back and down.

6. Roll the centre across the folded ribbon to form the first petal.

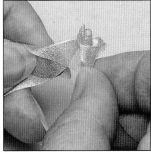

7. Pick up the dangling needle and work two stitches through all layers of ribbon at the base of the rose. Pull the thread through firmly.

8. Second petal. With your left thumb and forefinger, fold the top edge of the ribbon back and down again.

9. Roll the centre across the folded ribbon as before. Work two stitches through all layers at the base to secure the second petal.

10. Remaining petals. Continue folding, wrapping and stitching in the same manner until only 2cm ($^3/_4$") of ribbon remains.

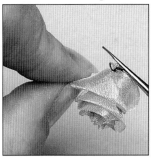

11. Final petal. Fold the ribbon back and down as before. Wrap the ribbon end around the base, forming a partial petal.

12. Securing the rose. Turn the rose upside down. Wind the thread around the base and take two stitches to secure. End off the thread.

13. Trim excess ribbon as close as possible to the base of the rose without cutting the stitching (approximately 2 - 3mm - $^1/_8$").

14. Completed folded ribbon rose.

Simple Pleasures

designed by Annie Humphris
of South Australia

OPULENT RED AND GOLD THREADS DECORATE THESE SHIMMERING BLACK BROCADE SPECTACLE CASES. THE COUCHED INITIALS ARE EMBELLISHED WITH GOLD THREAD BOWS AND THE LADY'S CASE HAS TWO RED ROSES. LINED IN RICH RED TAFFETA AND BOUND WITH BLACK SATIN BINDING, EACH IS FINISHED WITH A KEYHOLE TASSEL. CHOOSE YOUR OWN SPECIAL INITIAL FROM THE ALPHABET IN THE CENTRE LIFTOUT.

REQUIREMENTS

Fabric (for one case)
22cm square (8 ½") piece of black brocade

22cm square (8 ½") piece of red taffeta for lining

Threads & Needles
Madeira stranded cotton

A = 0210 Christmas red

Anchor Marlitt stranded rayon

B = 868 gold

C = 1011 lt khaki green

Madeira no. 40 metallic thread

D = 8 gold

No. 6 crewel needle

No. 8 crewel needle

No. 10 crewel needle

Supplies (for one case)
22cm square (8 ½") piece of thin wadding *(Pellon)*

50cm x 20mm wide (20" x ¾") black satin bias binding

THIS DESIGN USES:

Couching   French knot

Straight stitch   Detached chain

Detached blanket stitch

EMBROIDERY PREPARATION

See the centre liftout for the full-size pattern and entire alphabet embroidery designs.

Cutting out
Using the pattern in the centre liftout, cut one from each of the black brocade, lining fabric and wadding. Transfer all pattern markings to the black brocade fabric.

Transferring the design
Trace the initial of your choice onto tracing paper.

With wrong sides together, fold the brocade fabric into the shape of the case. Position the initial in the centre of the front section, aligning it with the placement marks transferred from the pattern.

Unfold the case and pin the tracing in position through one layer of fabric only *(diag 1)*.

Using the contrasting machine sewing thread, tack around the initial. Carefully tear the paper away, leaving the outline of the initial tacked onto the fabric.

Diag 1

EMBROIDERY

Dramatic in red and gold, the initials on these stunning spectacle cases are created from couched threads. A simple gold bow decorates the masculine version. Two long-stemmed rosebuds tied with a similar gold bow decorate the feminine version.

Initial
Using the no. 6 crewel needle and six strands of red thread, bring the thread to the front at the beginning of one section of the initial. Couch it in place along the tacked lines with tiny gold straight stitches. Remove the tacking as you stitch. Work the remaining sections in the same manner.

Rosebuds
The petals of each rosebud are three straight stitches that start from the same point at the base and fan out. Work a tiny straight stitch at the tip of the petals in green thread, splitting the end of the centre red stitch. Starting at the base, add a detached chain on either side for sepals and a french knot at the centre of the base for the calyx. The stems are single long straight stitches held in place by the bow at their centres.

Bow

Embroider three straight stitches in the same manner as the rosebuds for each bow loop. Add a french knot for the bow knot. Finish the bow with 3 to 4 straight stitches in metallic thread laid over the bow loops.

EMBROIDERY KEY

All embroidery is worked with one strand of thread unless otherwise specified.

Initial = A (6 strands, laid thread), B (4 strands, couching)

Rosebuds

Petals = A (6 strands, straight stitch)

Tip = C (straight stitch)

Sepals = C (detached chain)

Calyx = C (french knot, 1 wrap)

Stems = C (straight stitch)

Bow

Bow loops = B (6 strands, straight stitch)

Bow knot = B (6 strands, french knot, 1 wrap)

Highlights = D (straight stitch)

CONSTRUCTION

See pages 29 and 29 for step-by-step instructions for assembling the spectacle case and constructing the keyhole tassel.

STEP-BY-STEP
STITCH INSTRUCTIONS NOT
INCLUDED IN THIS ARTICLE
CAN BE FOUND ON THE
FOLLOWING PAGES.

→→❈←←

Straight stitch - page 46
French knot - page 40
Detached chain - page 46

COUCHING

1. Bring the base thread to the front at the beginning of the line. Lay it on the fabric along the line to be covered. Bring the second thread to the front next to the laid thread.

2. Take the second thread to the back over the laid thread.

3. Pull the thread through, forming a very short straight stitch. Re-emerge a short distance along the laid thread.

4. Continue couching the laid thread along the line in the same manner. When nearing the end, take the laid thread to the back. Complete the couching stitches. End off both threads on the back.

Larger than actual size

KEYHOLE TASSEL

One tiny tassel created from cotton, rayon and metallic threads is attached to the front of the spectacle case after it is completely assembled.

The head of the tassel is fashioned into a keyhole with detached blanket stitch.

1. Forming the tassel. Cut two pieces of card, each 4cm square (1 1/2"). Cut 3 lengths of thread (one each of A, B and D), 25cm (10") long. Place the threads together and wind around the two pieces of card three times.

2. With a small piece of spare thread, tie the threads together at the top between the two pieces of card. Cut the threads at the bottom between the pieces of card.

3. Using two long strands of A, tightly wrap the neck several times approximately 8mm (5/16") from the top.

4. Working the detached blanket stitch keyhole. Thread the two strands onto a needle. Take the needle through the wraps around the neck to secure it.

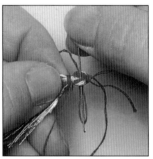

5. Holding the thread in the left hand, take the eye of the needle through the keyhole. Ensure the loop of thread is under the needle.

6. Begin to pull the thread through the keyhole and the loop.

7. Pull very tightly so a ridge forms on the outer edge of the keyhole. **Completed first detached blanket stitch.**

8. Continue to work the detached blanket stitches until reaching the tie at the top. Remove the tie.

9. Continue stitching until the entire keyhole is completely covered with stitches. Wrap the remaining thread around the neck of the tassel three times.

10. Take the needle through the neck to the other side. Repeat 2 - 3 times to secure the thread.

11. Take the needle though the neck and emerge in the skirt. The excess thread becomes part of the skirt.

12. Trim the length of the skirt to 3cm (1 1/4"). **Completed tassel.**

CONSTRUCTION OF THE SPECTACLE CASE

The spectacle case is lined in rich red taffeta and bound with black satin binding. The case is assembled after the embroidery is worked.

We used contrasting thread and binding for photographic purposes only.

1. Place the lining face down. Position the wadding on top and then the brocade fabric with the right side uppermost. Pin the three layers together around the outside.

2. Tack around all sides to prevent movement.

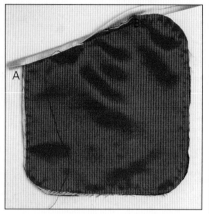

3. With brocade fabric facing you and right sides together, pin and stitch the binding from A to B. Trim seam. Leave excess binding extending. Fold the binding over the raw edges. Starting at A, slipstitch in place for 5cm (2").

4. Fold the spectacle case in half along the fold line. Pin binding from B, down the side and along the base. Trim excess binding 1cm (3/8") beyond the fold. At the lower edge, turn in the raw end of the binding level with the case. Stitch from B to the fold, through all layers.

5. Fold the binding over the raw edges of the case and pin. Stitch neatly in place by hand. Slipstitch the open end of the binding together at the fold.

6. Attach the finished tassel to the top right hand corner of the front. **Completed spectacle case.**

Created by Jennifer Newman of New South Wales

A celebration of the senses.
A delicate scented sachet of pink roses.

The

Maiden's

Blush

Shimmering pink roses created from cast-on stitch are clustered on the front of this dainty scented sachet.
The scallop-edged sachet is made from tucked silk dupion and ties with a satin-edged organza ribbon.

REQUIREMENTS

Fabric
56cm x 20cm wide (22" x 8") piece of ivory silk dupion

Threads & Needle
Lola Brazilian embroidery thread
A = 004 variegated pale pink
B = 153 med pink
C = 216 green
Sulky 40 machine sewing thread
D = 942-1113 pale pink
No. 3 straw (milliner's) needle

Supplies
Mokuba no. 4546 crepe georgette ribbon 25mm wide (1")
1m (40") no. 31 pink
10cm x 15cm wide (4" x 6") piece of fabric stabiliser (Tearaway)
Small amount of potpourri
Water-soluble fabric marker

PREPARATION FOR EMBROIDERY

See the centre liftout for the simplified embroidery design, full-size pattern and pintucking template.

Pintucking the fabric
Place the left half of the fabric over the pintucking template and trace the lines using a ruler and water-soluble fabric marker. Repeat for the right half, matching the lines with the previous half.

Stitch the tucks, working all the lines in one direction before stitching the lines in the other direction. Keep the stitching 1mm ($1/16$") from the fold.

Transferring the design
Trace the pattern, including all the markings and the embroidery design onto tracing paper.

Pin the tracing to the right side of the fabric, matching the marked diamonds on the tracing the pintucked diamonds.

Using a large needle, pierce holes in the tracing to mark the positions of the roses.

Dot each hole with the fabric marker and remove the tracing.

EMBROIDERY

The three roses and their leaves are worked entirely in cast-on stitch with the straw needle. Embroider the roses first, finishing one rose before beginning the next.

The centre of each rose is one stitch of twelve cast-ons. This cast-on stitch is worked over a tiny distance of approximately 3mm ($1/8$") so it forms a loop.

A round of five overlapping cast-on stitches forms the inner petals.

The outer petals are formed from 7 to 9 cast-on stitches that overlap in the same manner as the inner round of petals.

Two cast-on stitches are used to create each set of leaves. These two stitches are worked closely together to give the impression of overlapping leaves.

EMBROIDERY KEY

All embroidery is worked using one strand of thread.

Rose
Centre = B (1 cast-on stitch, 12 cast-ons)
Inner petals = A (5 cast-on stitches, 16 cast-ons)
Outer petals = A (7 - 9 cast-on stitches, 19 cast-ons)

Leaves
Inner leaves = C (1 cast-on stitch, 12 cast-ons)
Outer leaves = C (1 cast-on stitch, 14 cast-ons)

Scallops = D (machine satin stitch)

THIS DESIGN USES:

Cast-on stitch

CONSTRUCTION

See below for step-by-step instructions for the machine-embroidered scallops.

Once all embroidery is complete, rinse the fabric in cold water to remove any traces of the fabric marker. Dry flat and press lightly on the right side, avoiding the embroidery. Work the scalloped edge before assembling the sachet.

Sewing the side seams

French seams are used to assemble the sachet. With wrong sides together, fold the fabric in half along the foldline.

Using straight stitch, machine stitch along both sides 6mm (1/4") from the raw edges. Trim the seam allowances to 2 to 3mm (1/8") and press well. Turn the sachet to the wrong side and press the seams. Stitch 4mm (3/16") from the previous lines of stitching, enclosing the raw edges within the stitching. Press.

Finishing off

Turn to the right side and press. Fill the sachet with potpourri.

Tie the ribbon in a bow around the neck of the sachet. Trim the ends diagonally.

MACHINE-EMBROIDERED SCALLOPS

The scallops are machine-embroidered using white sewing thread in the bobbin and the Sulky machine embroidery thread (D) for the top thread. Some sewing machines have a pre-set scallop stitch and this can be used rather than the following method. Use an open embroidery foot and tighten the bobbin tension slightly. We recommend you practise on a sample first.

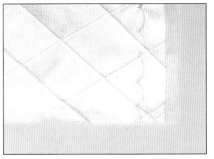

1. Cut the piece of fabric stabilizer in half. Place one piece under the marked scallops on one end of the fabric.

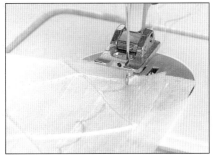

2. Use a very close zigzag or satin stitch. Lower the needle into the fabric on the right side of the line.

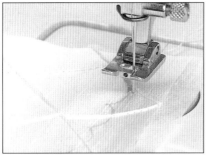

3. Lower the foot. Begin stitching very slowly, following the curve of the scallop. Stop frequently with the needle down on right side of the line to turn the fabric.

4. When reaching the point between two scallops, stop with the needle in the fabric to the left side of the scallops. Lift the foot, reposition the fabric ready to stitch the next scallop.

5. Continue stitching slowly and carefully along the scalloped line to the end of the fabric. Remove the fabric stabiliser and carefully trim excess fabric away from the scallops.

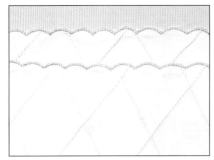

6. Work the scallops on the other end of the fabric in the same manner. **Completed scallops.**

CAST-ON STITCH ROSE

These beautiful roses are created entirely from three rounds of cast-on stitches. One stitch forms the centre, five stitches form the second round and seven to nine stitches are used for the third round.

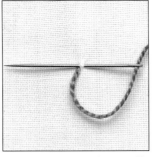

1. Centre. Bring the needle to the front 2mm (¹/₁₆") to the left of centre. Insert the needle 3mm (¹/₈") to the right. Re-emerge at the first point. Leave needle in fabric.

2. With palm facing you and the thread to the left, place the thread over your left index finger.

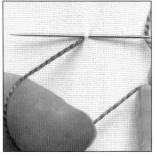

3. Rotate your hand towards you in a clockwise direction. Keep the thread taut and looped over your index finger.

4. Continue to rotate your hand until the thread is wrapped around your finger.

5. Keeping tension on the thread, place the tip of your finger on the point of the needle.

6. Slip the loop off your finger and onto the needle.

7. Pull the thread tight and slip the loop down the needle onto the fabric. This is the first cast-on.

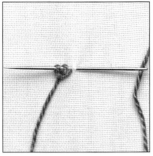

8. Work a second cast-on in the same manner. Position it on the needle alongside the first.

9. Work ten more cast-ons onto the needle.

10. Hold the cast-ons in your left hand. With your right hand, pull the needle and thread through them.

11. To anchor the stitch, take the needle to the back close to where the needle last emerged.

12. Pull the thread through. Pull firmly but do not let the fabric pucker. End off the thread. **Completed centre.**

Each set of leaves is two overlapping cast-on stitches. Turn the fabric as you work.

It is important to keep a consistent tension on the cast-ons as you work. Ensure they sit side-by-side on the needle and are even on the needle.

We used DMC pearl no.8 cotton for photographic purposes only.

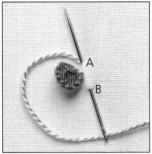

13. Inner petals. Bring the needle to the front at A. Insert the needle at B and re-emerge at A, leaving the needle in the fabric.

14. Follow steps 2 - 8 and then work 14 more cast-ons.

15. Holding the cast-ons with your left hand, pull the needle and thread through them with your right hand.

16. Anchor the stitch at B in the same manner as before.

17. Bring the needle to the front at C. Take it from D to C leaving the needle in the fabric.

18. Work a second stitch with 16 cast-ons in same manner as before. Work three more stitches, each with 16 cast-ons, to complete inner round.

19. Outer petals. Bring the needle to the front just underneath one petal of the inner round of petals.

20. Work 7 - 9 overlapping stitches in the same manner with 19 cast-ons in each stitch to complete the outer round of petals.

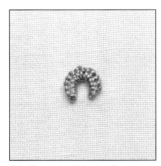

21. Leaves. Stitch the outer leaf first, using 14 cast-ons and with the two points where the needle pierces the fabric approximately 4mm (³/16") apart.

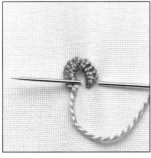

22. Bring the needle to the front, between the ends of the previous stitch. Take the needle through the fabric just beyond the first leaf and re-emerge at the first point.

23. Stitch the inner leaf using 12 cast-ons.

24. Work two sets of leaves alongside each rose. **Completed cast-on stitch rose.**

by Phil Drew of Victoria

JOURNEY'S END

Slightly exotic in their shape and design, these aromatic shoe fillers will keep a suitcase smelling sweet whilst helping shoes retain their shape.

A perfect gift for the seasoned traveller.

*Whimsical berries and leaves are stitched on the
front of the white damask fillers in luminous pearl thread.
A handful of sweet smelling lavender mixes with the filling.
The tops are finished with satin binding and tie with sage green ribbons.*

REQUIREMENTS FOR ONE PAIR

Fabric
30cm x 70cm wide (12" x 27 $^1/_2$")
piece of white damask

Threads & Needle
DMC pearl no. 8 cotton
A = 503 med blue-green
DMC pearl no. 5 cotton
B = 223 lt shell pink
C = 309 deep rose
D = 368 lt pistachio green
E = 503 med blue-green
No. 22 chenille needle

Supplies
70cm x 25mm wide (27 $^1/_2$" x 1")
white satin bias binding
1m x 7mm wide (40" x $^5/_{16}$")
sage green satin ribbon
50g (2oz) polyester fibre-fill
Small amount of dried lavender
10cm x 20cm wide (4" x 8")
piece of lightweight fusible
interfacing
Sharp lead pencil

PATTERN & CUTTING OUT

*See the centre liftout for the full-size
pattern and cutting layout.*

From the damask cut four pieces,
two for each shoe filler.

EMBROIDERY PREPARATION

*See the centre liftout for the
embroidery designs.*

Transferring the designs

Trace the embroidery design and
cutting lines for each shoe filler
onto tracing paper.

Matching the cutting lines on the
tracing with the raw edges of the
fabric, place the embroidery
design over one piece of damask.
Pin in place to prevent movement.

Using a large needle, pierce holes
in the tracing along the lines of
the design at 2 to 3mm ($^1/_8$")
intervals. Make a pencil mark
through each hole in the paper.
Remove the tracing. Repeat for
the other shoe filler.

Applying the interfacing

Cut the piece of interfacing in
half. Iron one piece onto the
wrong side of one front behind
the marked design. Iron the
remaining piece to the other
front in the same manner.

EMBROIDERY

Each fragrant shoe filler is
embroidered with a large sprig
of berries, buds and leaves.
Embroidered entirely in pearl
cotton thread, the designs have a
lustrous sheen.

Stitch the four berries and three
buds, followed by all stems. The
three large leaves are stitched
next. The small leaves and calyxes
are added last.

Berries

Using the shell pink thread, fill
each berry shape with tightly
packed colonial knots.

Start from the base and work
towards the top. Fill in any spaces
around the edges with random
french knots.

Randomly add rose or green french
knots to some of the berries.

Stitch 2 - 6 satin stitches for each
segment of the calyxes.

Buds

Work 4 - 7 straight stitches in the
shell pink thread for each bud.
Start with the centre stitch and
work towards the sides.

Leaves

Work the outlines for the large
leaves in back stitch.

Fill in the large side leaves in satin
stitch and then the large centre
leaf. Completely cover the back
stitch outlines with satin stitches.

The small leaves are formed from
1 - 5 satin stitches.

Stems

The thick stem is embroidered in
satin stitch, starting from its base
and working towards the leaves.

All other stems are stitched in
stem stitch.

CONSTRUCTION

All seam allowances are 1cm
($^3/_8$") unless otherwise specified.

With right sides together and
matching raw edges, place each
embroidered front onto the
corresponding back.

Stitch around both
sides of each filler.
Pivot at the point.

Neaten seams.
Clip the seam
allowance at the
curves and point
(*diag 1*). Press the
seams open.
Turn to the right side.

Diag 1

Cut the length of satin bias binding in half. Fold under one end of the binding. With edges even and right sides together, pin the binding to the top of one shoe filler starting with the unfolded end. Lap the second end over the first (diag 2).

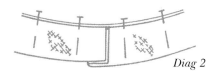

Diag 2

Stitch. Fold the binding to the wrong side and slipstitch in place. Carefully press. Repeat for the second shoe filler.

Stitch a row of hand gathering stitches around each shoe filler 7cm (2 ³/₄") down from the top edge (diag 3).

Diag 3

Half fill one shoe filler with the polyester fibre-fill, packing it down firmly. Place half the lavender inside. Continue filling until reaching the line of gathering. Draw up the gathering thread and tie firmly. Pack the second shoe filler in the same manner.

Cut the green satin ribbon in half. Tie one piece in a bow around the gathering on each shoe filler.

> STEP-BY-STEP
> STITCH INSTRUCTIONS NOT
> INCLUDED IN THIS ARTICLE
> CAN BE FOUND ON THE
> FOLLOWING PAGES.
>
> Back stitch - page 70
> Satin stitch - page 9
> Stem stitch - page 46
> Straight stitch - page 46

EMBROIDERY KEY

All embroidery is worked with one strand of thread.

Berries

Berries = B (colonial knot),
A and C (french knot, 1 wrap)
Calyxes = E (satin stitch)
Buds = B (straight stitch)

Leaves

Large centre leaf = A
(back stitch), E (satin stitch)
Large side leaves = A (back stitch),
D (satin stitch)
Small leaves = E (satin stitch)

Stems

Thick stem = D (satin stitch)
Thin stems = D (stem stitch)

JOURNEY'S END

THIS DESIGN USES:

Back stitch	*Satin stitch*
Colonial knot	*Stem stitch*
French knot	*Straight stitch*

FRENCH KNOT

A french knot is a raised stitch.

Traditionally it was worked with only one wrap on the needle but today it is often worked with more than one wrap.

A larger knot will look neater worked with more strands of thread rather than too many wraps.

Always wrap with the needle pointing away from the fabric.

We used pearl no. 3 cotton for photographic purposes only.

1. Secure the thread on the back of the work. Bring the thread to the front.

2. Hold the thread firmly with your left thumb and index finger 3cm (1 ¼") away from the fabric.

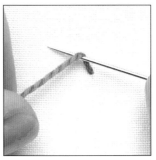

3. With the left hand, take the thread over the needle. Ensure the needle points away from the fabric.

4. Wrap the thread under and over the needle. Keeping the thread taut, begin to twist the needle away from you, taking the point of the needle towards the fabric.

5. Take the needle through the fabric approx 1 - 2 fabric threads away from where the thread came up.

6. Slide the knot onto the fabric. Pull until the knot is firm around the needle.

7. Slowly push the needle to the wrong side of the fabric while holding the knot in place with your thumb.

8. Continue pulling until the loop disappears under your thumb and the thread is completely pulled through. **Completed French knot.**

HINTS ON FRENCH & COLONIAL KNOTS

1. Always slide the wraps down onto the fabric before pulling the needle and thread through. This prevents unwanted loops from forming.

2. Ensure you do not take the thread to the back through exactly the same hole in the fabric. As you pull firmly it will disappear.

COLONIAL KNOT

Also known as candlewicking knots, colonial knots are slightly larger and more raised than french knots. They are a very secure knot.

Each is worked as a figure eight in two stages.

We used pearl no. 3 cotton for photographic purposes only.

1. Secure the thread on the back of the fabric. Bring to the front at the desired position for the knot.

2. Hold the thread away from the fabric with your left hand. With the right hand, take the needle towards the fabric and thread (over the thread).

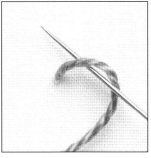

3. Hook the needle under the thread where it emerges from the fabric.

4. Shorten the loop. With your left hand, take the thread over the tip of the needle.

5. Take the thread under the tip of the needle. The thread now forms a figure eight over the needle.

6. Take the tip of the needle to the back, approx 1 - 2 fabric threads away from where it emerged.

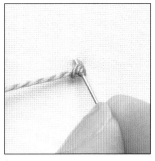

7. Pull the wraps tight against the fabric and begin to take the needle through the fabric.

8. Keeping the thread taut, push the needle through the wraps to the back of the fabric.

9. Holding the knot in place with your thumb, pull the thread through from the back of the fabric (thumb not shown).

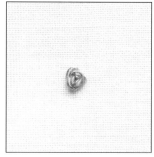

10. Completed colonial knot.

THE ORIGINS OF CANDLEWICKING

Candlewicking had its beginnings in America in the early 1800's.

The pioneer women used a cotton twist yarn that was used in candle making as their thread, hence the name.

It is an easy yet effective form of embroidery.

French and colonial knots are the basic stitches used, but satin, stem and and back stitch have also been traditionally used.

An elegant coffee
plunger cover
designed by
Maree Moscato
of Victoria

Dolce Vita

A quietly elegant coffee plunger presiding with grace over the tea table. Sunny yellow and white shasta daisies dance across the checked cosy which is lined with batting and cotton twill. Blue piping finishes the edge and there is a top opening for the plunger.

REQUIREMENTS

Fabric

50cm x 115cm wide (20" x 45") checked cotton

40cm x 115cm wide (15 ³/₄" x 45") cotton twill for lining

Threads & Needles

DMC pearl no. 5 cotton

A = white

B = 444 dk lemon

C = 502 blue-green

No. 18 chenille needle

Supplies

40cm x 115cm wide (15 ³/₄" x 45") polyester batting

1m x 3.5cm wide (40" x 1 ³/₈") blue bias tape

1m (40") size 0 piping cord

Water-soluble fabric marker

THIS DESIGN USES:

Colonial knot   Detached chain
Back stitch   Stem stitch
Straight stitch

EMBROIDERY PREPARATION

See the centre liftout for the full-size pattern and embroidery design.

Trace the pattern, including the embroidery design and all markings, onto tracing paper.

Place the tracing onto the right side of the checked fabric ensuring the checks are centred with the pattern design.

Pin in place to prevent movement. Cut out the front along the marked cutting lines.

Using a large needle, pierce holes in the tracing along the lines of the design and pattern markings at 2 - 3mm (¹/₈") intervals. Dot each hole with the fabric marker.

Overcast all edges on the sewing machine.

EMBROIDERY

Sunny yellow and white shasta daisies decorate the front of this cheery coffee plunger cover.

A long twirling stem-stitched ribbon loosely ties the slender stems of the daisies.

Stitch the flowers and ribbon, followed by the stems. The leaves are added last.

All embroidery is worked with one strand of thread and the chenille needle.

Daisies

The petals are worked from the outside to the centre in a random order. Three to seven closely worked colonial knots form each centre.

Ribbon

The outline of the yellow ribbon is worked first in stem stitch. Embroider the ribbon folds in back stitch. Start at the centre and stitch towards the ends of the ribbon.

Stems and leaves

Using the green thread, embroider all stems in stem stitch.

Add the leaves last, varying the length of the anchoring stitch on the detached chains.

CONSTRUCTION

See the centre liftout.

EMBROIDERY KEY

*All embroidery is worked using
one strand of thread.*

Daisies

Centre = A or B
(3 - 7 colonial knots)

Petals = A or B
(16 - 50 straight stitches)

Leaves = C (detached chain)

Stems = C (stem stitch)

Ribbon

Outline = B (stem stitch)

Folds = B (back stitch)

STEP-BY-STEP
STITCH INSTRUCTIONS
NOT INCLUDED IN THIS
ARTICLE CAN BE FOUND ON
THE FOLLOWING PAGES.

Back stitch - page 70

Colonial knot - page 41

STRAIGHT STITCH FLOWER

Straight stitch can be used in a large variety of ways and is often combined with other stitches.

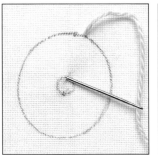 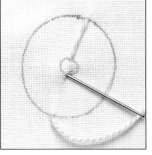  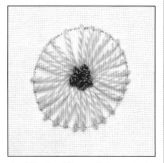

1. Bring the thread to the front on the outer edge of the flower. Take it to the back at the centre mark to complete the straight stitch.

2. Re-emerge on the outer edge opposite the first stitch. Take the needle to the back at the centre mark.

3. Continue working stitches, varying their length slightly and always working stitches roughly opposite each other.

4. Work 16 to 50 straight stitches. Add 3 to 7 colonial knots for the centre. **Completed straight stitch flower.**

STEM STITCH

Stem stitch is similar in appearance to outline stitch. The thread is always kept below the needle, whereas in outline stitch it is always kept above.

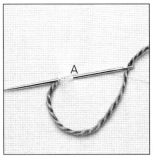 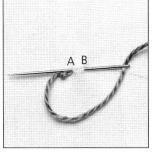 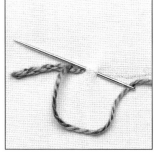 

1. Bring the needle to the front at one end of the marked line. With the thread below the needle, take the needle to the back at A. Re-emerge at the end of the line.

2. Pull the thread through. Again with the thread below the needle, take the needle from B to A.

3. Pull the thread through. Continue working stitches in the same manner, always keeping the thread below the needle and the stitches the same size.

4. To end off, take the needle to the back for the last stitch but do not re-emerge. Secure the thread on the back with tiny back stitches. **Completed stem stitch.**

DETACHED CHAIN

Detached chain is a looped stitch which can be worked individually or in groups. It combines readily with other stitches.

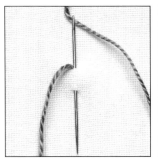   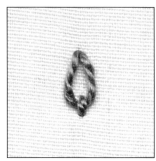

1. Bring the needle to the front at the base of the stitch. Take the needle to the back just to the right of where you came up and re-emerge at the tip of the stitch.

2. Take the thread under the point of the needle in an anti-clockwise direction to form a loop.

3. Keeping your left thumb over the loop, pull the thread through. The tighter you pull, the thinner the stitch will become (thumb not shown).

4. To anchor the stitch, take the thread over the loop and to the back. **Completed detached chain.**

TRANSFERRING EMBROIDERY DESIGNS

The question of how to transfer designs onto fabric to be embroidered has taxed the ingenuity of embroiderers for hundreds of years. During the 17th and 18th centuries, designs were generally drawn directly onto the fabric by professional artists using a pen or brush. Many methods have been tried since then. The result depends on the type of fabric or the particular embroidery technique to be used.

TACKING (BASTING)

This method is time consuming but is the most satisfactory of all the methods as it leaves no permanent mark. Work can be left without fear of the design being erased or the fabric damaged. Designs can be altered as work progresses.

Using a fine tipped pen, trace the design onto tissue or baking paper. Pin the tracing, design uppermost, onto the right side of the fabric.

With fine sewing thread in a contrasting colour, work small, even tacking stitches through the paper and fabric, following the design lines.

When tacking is completed, score the tracing lines with a needle and gently tear the paper away.

Remove the tacking as you work your embroidery stitches.

FABRIC MARKERS

Fabric markers which are either water-soluble or fade with time are available.

The disappearing markers fade entirely within approximately 48 hours. Use with caution for heirloom garments and projects. These markers are spirit-based and may cause the fabric to deteriorate over a period of time.

Water-soluble marks are removed by dabbing or rinsing in cold water. Remove the marks before applying heat (eg ironing) as this will make them permanent and can cause discoloration of the fabric.

Never use felt-tipped or ball-point pens meant for writing on paper.

If the fabric becomes permanently marked, it is essential to cover the marks in some way.

DIRECT TRACING

This method is used if the design can be seen through the fabric. First, draw the design onto paper using black ink or a felt-tipped pen. Place the design under the fabric on a flat surface. Smooth the fabric and tape both the fabric and the paper to the surface with masking tape.

Using a sharpened dressmaker's pencil, a lead pencil or a fabric marker, trace the design directly onto the fabric.

It is sometimes possible to tape the design and fabric to a window during daylight or an illuminated light box, to make the lines more visible. The light shining though the fabric will emphasise the design and make it easier to follow.

PRICKING THE TRACING

Trace the embroidery design onto tracing paper and place over the right side of the fabric in the required position. Pin or tape the design to the fabric to prevent movement.

Using a large needle, pierce holes in the tracing at approximately 6mm (¼") intervals along the lines, or pierce holes for certain features in the design as required.

Using a chalk marker or water-soluble pen, mark the fabric through each hole in the paper. Remove the tracing. You may wish to draw a connecting line through the dots for the lines.

DRESSMAKER'S CARBON

This method can be used for heavier or opaque fabrics. The carbon paper comes in a variety of colours, so choose one which will show on the background fabric but blend with the colour of the embroidery.

Spread the fabric onto a flat smooth surface and tape to prevent movement. Place the carbon paper on top, waxed side down. Finally place the traced design in position and hold in place with tape.

Draw the design lines using a sharp, hard lead pencil or a tracing wheel. Note: typewriter carbon paper must never be used.

Rambling Rose

A classic design capturing

the essence of romance.

The enchanting wool beret is

discretely embroidered with

blossoms and buds.

CREATED BY CAROLYN PEARCE

OF NEW SOUTH WALES

Three pale peach apple blossoms and two buds are surrounded with sweet william and forget-me-nots on the front of the beret.

Made from pure wool blanketing, the romantic beret is lined with ivory slipper satin. Cream grosgrain ribbon finishes the inner edge to prevent stretching.

The beret is designed to fit a head with a circumference of 56cm (22").

REQUIREMENTS

Fabric

40cm x 75cm wide (16" x 29 $^1/_2$") piece of white pure wool blanketing

40cm x 75cm wide (16" x 29 $^1/_2$") piece of ivory slipper satin

Threads & Needles

Appletons 2 ply crewel wool

A = 101 pale purple

B = 353 grey-green

C = 471 lt autumn yellow

D = 695 honeysuckle yellow

E = 751 lt rose pink

F = 877 pale peach

G = 886 pastel blue

DMC Broder Médici

H = 8405 sage green

Kirra Yarn 2 ply mohair

I = 118 olive

DMC stranded cotton

J = 3721 dk shell pink

K = 3740 dk antique violet

Rajmahal Art silk

L = 45 baby camel

M = 121 bluebell

N = 421 green earth

Waterlilies by Caron
- variegated stranded silk

O = olive

Needle Necessities Floss

P = 189 kismet

Kacoonda variegated mohair

Q = 6C dusky earth

No. 22 chenille needle

No. 5 crewel needle

No. 8 crewel needle

Supplies

40cm square (16") piece of woven lightweight fusible interfacing

58cm x 2.5cm wide (22 $^3/_4$" x 1") cream grosgrain ribbon

10cm x 20cm wide (4" x 8") piece of tulle

Black fine tip permanent marker

Water-soluble fabric marker

CUTTING OUT

See the centre liftout for the full-size pattern and cutting layout.

Cut out the upper and lower sections of the beret from the blanketing. The hole for the head is cut from the lower section after the embroidery is complete.

Before removing the pattern, tailor's tack the midpoints on both sections of the beret.

Use different coloured threads to indicate the centre front and centre back (diag 1).

Diag 1 — Midpoint / Midpoint

Cut one upper section and one lower section from the satin for the lining and cut one lower section from the interfacing.

EMBROIDERY PREPARATION

See the centre liftout for the embroidery design.

Fuse the interfacing to the wrong side of the wool blanketing lower section.

The embroidery design is worked in the top left quarter of the lower section of the beret.

Baste along the seam lines in this quarter so you don't embroider into the seam allowance (diag 2).

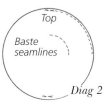

Diag 2 — Top / Baste seamlines

Transferring the design

Trace the design and placement markings onto the tulle with the fine black marker. Allow to dry thoroughly.

Place the tulle onto the right side of the blanketing in the basted quarter, aligning the placement markings. Ensure the overall design is centred between the seam allowances. Pin the tulle in place. Using the water-soluble fabric marker, trace the embroidery design, marking the stems and the centres of the flowers.

EMBROIDERY

Three pale peach apple blossoms and two delicate buds are surrounded with sweet violets and forget-me-nots on the front of the beret.

Use the no. 5 crewel needle for stitching the petals of the violets and forget-me-nots. The no. 8 crewel needle is used when stitching with 1 - 2 strands of cotton or silk. All other embroidery is stitched with the chenille needle.

Apple blossoms

Each petal is created from straight stitches using the same holes in the fabric.

Take care to ensure the stitches sit to the left or right of the centre stitch exactly. The petals should just touch for about 3mm (1/8") out from the base.

Start and finish the fly stitch slightly underneath the petal. This will ensure it really hugs the tips. Couch the stems in place and then work the fly stitch leaves.

Buds

Each bud is stitched in the same way as a blossom petal using approximately six stitches.

Starting at the centre base, work four straight stitches of different lengths over the bud for the sepals. The calyx is formed from eight straight stitches.

Couch stems in place. Overlay the bud with a few straight stitches in one strand of silk thread. Two fly stitches extend beyond the tip of the bud. Whip the stems with silk thread.

Violets

Each petal has four straight stitches using the same holes at the top and bottom.

Work the upper petals so they are placed like rabbit's ears.

Next, work the outer lower petals so they just touch at the base but angle downwards.

The lower centre petal is slightly longer than the others.

A fly stitch hugs the tip of each petal tightly and a single straight stitch extends from the tip towards the centre of the petal.

Add the petal markings and three french knots for the centres.

The leaves are small straight stitches.

Forget-me-nots

Stitch the centre first, then the petals, forming the first three into a 'Y'.

Fill in the last two petals on either side of the base of the 'Y'.

The leaves are detached chain.

Highlight each one with a straight stitch, starting from the outside of the leaf and going back into the centre.

EMBROIDERY KEY

All embroidery is worked with one strand of thread unless otherwise specified.

Apple blossom

Petals = F (2 strands, 6 - 8 straight stitches)

Between petals = B (straight stitch)

Tips = E (straight stitch, fly stitch)

Centre = C blended with 2 strands of P (5 french knots, 2 wraps), D blended with 2 strands of J (3 french knots, 2 wraps)

Stems = I (split back stitch)

Leaves = Q (fly stitch, smocker's knot)

Buds

Petal = F (2 strands, 6 straight stitches)

Tip = O (2 fly stitches)

Sepals = H (4 straight stitches)

Calyx = H (8 straight stitches)

Highlights on sepals and calyx = O (straight stitch)

Stems = H (couching), O (whipping)

Violets

Petals = A (4 straight stitches)

Tips = K (fly stitch, straight stitch)

Centre = J blended with L (1 strand of each, 3 colonial knots)

Lower petal markings = L (2 strands, straight stitch)

Leaves = O (straight stitch)

Forget-me-nots

Petals = G blended with M (1 strand of each, 5 colonial knots)

Centre = L (2 strands, 1 colonial knot)

Leaves = H (detached chain)

Leaf highlights = N (straight stitch)

Rambling Rose

STEP-BY-STEP
STITCH INSTRUCTIONS NOT
INCLUDED IN THIS ARTICLE
CAN BE FOUND ON THE
FOLLOWING PAGES.

Colonial knot - page 41
Couching - page 27
Detached chain - page 46
French knot - page 40
Straight stitch - page 46

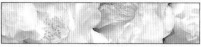

THIS DESIGN USES:

Detached chain   *Smocker's knot*
Colonial knot   *Straight stitch*
Couching   *French knot*
Fly stitch   *Whipping*
Split back stitch

CONSTRUCTING THE BERET

All seam allowances are 1cm ($^3/8$") unless otherwise specified.

Shaping the lower section

When the embroidery is complete, cut out the inner circle using the pattern as a guide. Using a gathering stitch, sew around the inner edge just inside the seam allowance *(diag 1)*.

Joining the upper and lower beret

With right sides together and matching mid points, pin the upper section to the lower section and stitch along the seamline. Stitch again 6mm ($^1/4$") away in the seam allowance *(diag 2)*.

Lining

With right sides together, pin the upper section to the lower section. Stitch the two layers together. Trim the seam allowance.

Joining the beret and lining

With wrong sides together and matching midpoints, pin the lining to the beret around the lower edge.

Tack and stitch the two layers together. Trim the seam allowance to 6mm ($^1/4$") *(diag 3)*.

Attaching the ribbon

With right sides together, join the ribbon into a circle.

Neaten the seam allowances and press open.

Starting at the centre back, pin the grosgrain ribbon to the seam allowance of the lower section, placing the lower edge of the ribbon along the seam line. Ease the blanketing to fit. *(diag 4)*.

Tack and stitch the ribbon in place. Clip the seam allowance of the lower section of the beret where necessary. Press.

Fold the ribbon to the inside and catch it to the lining with a few small stitches at the mid-points *(diag 5)*. Remove all tacking.

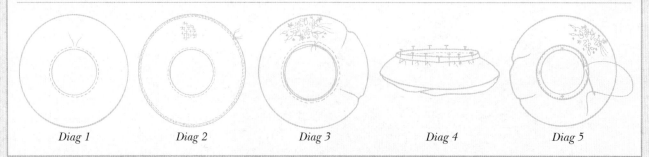

Diag 1   Diag 2   Diag 3   Diag 4   Diag 5

APPLE BLOSSOM

These beautiful blossoms are formed by combining straight stitches, fly stitches and french knots.

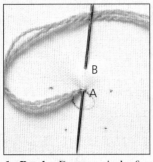

1. Petals. Draw a circle for the centre of the blossom. Mark five dots for the outside of the petals. Bring the needle to the front at A. Take a stitch from B to A.

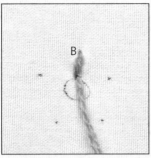

2. Gently pull the thread through. The inner point of each petal is on the circle.

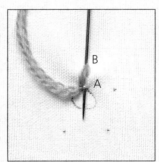

3. Take a second stitch from B to A with the thread to the left of the needle.

4. Pull the needle through. Leaving thread loose, place needle under thread as stitch is positioned. This helps to keep each stitch even and to create a 'plump' petal.

5. Pull the thread through, positioning the needle beneath the stitch, until the second stitch lies to the left, and snug against, the first stitch.

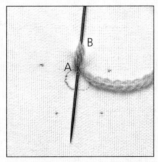

6. Remove the needle from under the stitch. With the thread to the right, take a third stitch from B to A.

7. Pull the thread until the stitch lies to the right, and snug against, the first stitch.

8. Work 3 - 5 more stitches, in the same way. The last three stitches are laid over the petal. **Completed first petal.**

9. Work four more petals in the same manner. The petals just touch each other near the centre.

10. Straight stitches between petals. Change thread. Work a short straight stitch between each petal, from the centre out to where the petals separate.

11. Tip. Change thread. Work a straight stitch from the middle of a petal to the tip and then a fly stitch that hugs the petal. Anchor the fly stitch at the petal tip.

12. Centre. The centre is worked using blended threads. Work five french knots in the first combination and three french knots in the second combination.
Completed apple blossom.

SMOCKER'S KNOT

Smocker's knots are used to form part of the calyxes on the buds and at the base of each fly stitch leaf.

To work the smocker's knot on the leaves, the needle does not go through the fabric.

Instead, the knot is worked over the anchoring stitch of a fly stitch.

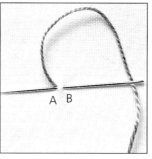

1. Bring thread to front at A. Take a back stitch from B to A, keeping thread above needle.

2. Pull the thread through leaving a small loop approx 1cm (³/8") in diameter.

3. Take the needle through the loop.

4. Pull the thread through leaving a second small loop approximately 1cm (³/8") in diameter.

5. Holding the thread in the left hand and the second loop in the right hand, begin to pull the second loop.

6. Pull until the first loop is tight and flat against the fabric. The second loop remains intact.

7. Take the needle through the remaining loop.

8. Begin to pull the thread through

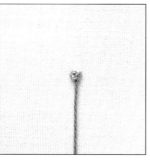

9. Pull the thread until the loops form a tight knot flat against the fabric.

10. Take the needle to the back under the knot to end off. **Completed smocker's knot.**

SPLIT BACK STITCH

In split back stitch, the needle splits the thread of the last stitch as it passes to the back of the fabric.

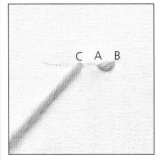

1. Bring the needle to the front at A. Pull the thread through. Take the needle to the back at B and re-emerge at C. Pull the thread through.

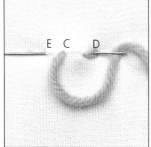

2. Take the needle to the back at D, splitting the threads of the previous stitch and re-emerge at E. **First completed split back stitch.**

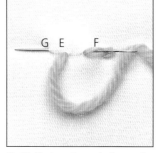

3. Pull the thread through. Take needle from F to G splitting second stitch as you take needle to back. Keep stitches even in length.

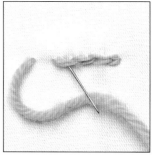

4. Continue in same manner to the end of the row. For the last stitch, take the needle to the back, splitting the previous stitch. End off.

FLY STITCH LEAF

Five to eight fly stitches with a smocker's knot at the base are used to form each leaf. The leaves can be made to curl either to the right or left.

We show a leaf curling to the left. For a leaf curling to the right, work the right hand side of each fly stitch shorter than the left hand side.

Draw a leaf shape with a centre vein onto the right side of the fabric.

1. Bring the needle to the front at A on the left hand side of the leaf near the tip.

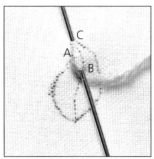

2. Take the needle to the back at B. Re-emerge at C on the centre vein.

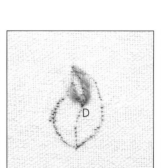

3. Pull the thread through. Take the needle to the back at D to anchor the fly stitch. **Completed first fly stitch.**

4. Work a second fly stitch just below first. Keep left side shorter than right side to ensure the leaf curls to left.

5. Work 3 - 6 more fly stitches down the leaf to fill the shape. The last stitch is anchored at the base.

6. Smocker's knot. Bring needle to front 1.5mm (1/16") away from base. Slide needle under last anchoring stitch.

7. Complete the knot following the instructions on the opposite page. **Completed fly stitch leaf.**

8. *Fly Stitch leaves as seen in Rambling Rose.*

WHIPPING

Whipping can be used with a multitude of stitches. Here it is worked over a couched thread.

1. Using a new thread, secure on the back of the fabric. Bring it to the front, just to the left of the foundation stitching.

2. Take the thread over the foundation stitches. Going from right to left, push eye of needle under. Do not go through fabric.

3. Pull the thread through. Take the thread over the line of stitches again. Push the eye of the needle under the third segment.

4. Pull the thread through. Continue working in the same manner to the end of the line. **Completed whipping.**

DELICATE BROOCHES WORKED IN SILK RIBBON AND THREAD

TREASURES

Designed by Liz Kulinski of South Australia
and Marjorie Kavanagh of Victoria

Two rounds of bullion knots surround the centre of this pretty brooch. A fitting symbol of love and friendship.

REQUIREMENTS

Fabric
15cm square (6") piece of ivory Honan silk

Threads & Needle
Madeira stranded silk
A = 0806 dk antique violet
B = 0812 med shell pink
C = 0813 lt shell pink
D = 0901 lt blue-violet
E = 1510 grey-green
F = 2207 vy lt old gold
No. 12 hand appliqué needle

Supplies
Purchased brooch finding
Small piece of thin wadding (Pellon)
Sharp lead pencil

EMBROIDERY PREPARATION
See the centre liftout for the embroidery design and pattern.

With the right side facing you, centre the piece of silk fabric over the pattern.

Using the lead pencil, carefully trace the cutting line and the shape of the garland.

Mark the centres of the roses with a dot and the positions of the bullion buds with a fine line.

EMBROIDERY
Stitch the stems first, using stem stitch. Start each one from the bottom and work towards the top carefully following the traced line.

All bullion roses are embroidered next, starting each one from the centre and working outwards.

Form the padded satin stitch centre of the large rose first.

Work four horizontal satin stitches overlaid with four vertical satin stitches. Surround the centre with two rounds of bullion knots.

Work a colonial knot for the centre of each small rose and encircle these with one round of bullion knots.

Embroider the bullion buds, their calyxes and the leaves.

The french knots, nestling among the roses, are added last.

CONSTRUCTION
See page 61 for step-by-step instructions for assembling the brooch.

THIS DESIGN USES:

French knot   Bullion knot
Straight stitch   Colonial knot
Stem stitch   Fly stitch
Padded satin stitch

EMBROIDERY KEY
All embroidery is worked using one strand of thread.

Large rose
Centre = B (padded satin stitch)
Inner petals = B (4 bullion knots, 6 wraps)
Outer petals = C (6 bullion knots, 8 wraps)

Small roses
Centre = B (colonial knot)
Petals = B or C (4 bullion knots, 6 wraps)
Pale pink bud = C (1 bullion knot, 6 wraps)
Sepal = E (fly stitch)

Yellow buds
Bud = F (2 bullion knots, 6 wraps)
Sepal = E (fly stitch)

Dark pink buds
Inner petal = B (1 bullion knot, 4 - 6 wraps)
Outer petals = C (fly stitch)

Stems and leaves
Stem = E (stem stitch)
Leaves = E (straight stitch)

Scattered french knots = A, C, D or F (french knot, 1 wrap)

BULLION KNOT

Bullion knots are raised stitches of twisted thread which nestle on the top of the fabric.

The distance between A and B is the length of the stitch.

You need enough wraps to cover this distance.

For a curved knot, add more wraps than are required to cover this distance.

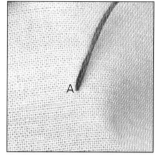

1. Bring the thread to the front at A and pull it through.

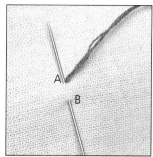

2. Take the needle to the back at B and re-emerge at A, taking care not to split the thread (thread is to right of needle). Leave needle in fabric.

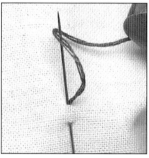

3. Place your left thumb on the eye of the needle to raise the tip of the needle in the air. Wrap the thread clockwise over the needle.

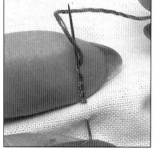

4. Pull the wrap firmly down onto the fabric. Continue wrapping in the same manner for the required number of wraps.

5. Keeping the thread taut, pack the wraps evenly down the needle onto the fabric.

6. Using your left index finger to keep tension on the wraps, begin to ease the needle and thread through the fabric and wraps.

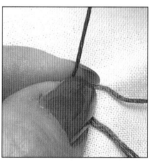

7. Holding the wraps firmly with your left thumb and index finger, continue pulling the thread through, pulling it away from you.

8. Pull the thread all the way through, tugging the wraps away from you (towards A). This helps ensure a tight, even stitch.

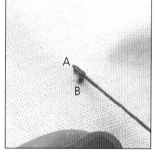

9. Keeping the thread taut, pull the thread firmly towards you (towards B). The knot now sits between A and B.

10. To ensure the wraps are even, gently stroke and manipulate them with the needle. Keep tension on the thread while doing this.

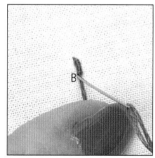

11. Anchor the knot by taking the needle to the back of the fabric at B.

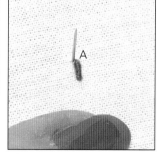

12. To work a 2 bullion bud, bring needle to front at A again. Use the same holes in the fabric to make the knots curve towards each other.

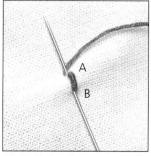

13. Pull the thread through. Insert the needle at B and re-emerge at A keeping the thread to the right hand side of the needle.

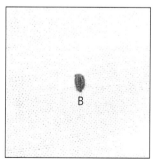

14. Complete the bullion knot in the same manner as for the first knot, anchoring it at B. **Completed bullion knot bud.**

THE SILK RIBBON BROOCH

Elegant pink fuchsias form the basis for the ribbon embroidery on this delightful little trinket. The brooch is assembled after the embroidery is worked.

REQUIREMENTS

Fabric

15cm square (6") piece of ivory silk dupion

Threads & Needles

YLI silk ribbon 4mm wide (³/16")

A = 25cm (10") no. 33 dk blue-green

B = 25cm (10") no. 127 lt pink

C = 40cm (16") no. 145 dk pink

Madeira stranded cotton

D = 0604 deep rose

E = 1314 dk hunter green

No. 24 chenille needle

No. 10 'sharp' needle

Supplies

Purchased brooch finding

Small piece of thin wadding *(Pellon)*

10cm (4") embroidery hoop

Sharp lead pencil

EMBROIDERY PREPARATION

See the centre liftout for the embroidery design and pattern.

With the right side facing you, centre the piece of silk fabric over the pattern.

THIS DESIGN USES:

Pistil stitch   Stem stitch
Ribbon stitch   Straight stitch

Using the lead pencil, carefully trace the pattern markings and the stems of the fuchsias.

Mark the positions of the leaves and petals with single lines.

EMBROIDERY

Begin by stitching the stems and straight stitch portions of the calyxes. Carefully place the fabric into the hoop with the design in the centre to work the remainder of the embroidery.

Using the pale pink ribbon, work two ribbon stitches very close together for the petals.

Starting each one from the base of the petals, stitch 4 - 5 ribbon stitches for each colourful calyx.

Five pistil stitches are placed at the tip of each flower. Begin with the long centre stamen. Stitch the remaining stamens on either side gradually decreasing their length as you work outwards.

Finally, embroider eight ribbon stitch leaves along the stems.

Use the 'sharp' needle for all thread embroidery and the chenille needle for all ribbon embroidery.

EMBROIDERY KEY

All thread embroidery is worked using one strand.

Fuchsias

Petals = B (ribbon stitch)

Calyx = C (ribbon stitch), E (straight stitch)

Stamens = D (pistil stitch)

Stems = E (stem stitch)

Leaves = A (ribbon stitch)

CONSTRUCTION

See opposite page for step-by-step instructions for assembling the brooch.

STEP-BY-STEP STITCH INSTRUCTIONS NOT INCLUDED IN THIS ARTICLE CAN BE FOUND ON THE FOLLOWING PAGES.

Colonial knot - page 41
Fly stitch - page 15
French knot - page 40
Padded satin stitch - page 9
Ribbon stitch - page 15
Stem stitch - page 46
Straight stitch - page 46

PISTIL STITCH

Pistil stitch is a french knot on a stem.

The length of the stem and the number of wraps on the knot depend on the desired effect.

Pistil stitches worked close together and in varying lengths are often used for flower stamens or petals.

For a curved effect, loosen the tension as you place the stitch for the stem.

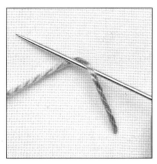

1. Secure the thread on the back of the fabric. Bring it to the front at the base of the stitch.

2. Holding the thread firmly with the left thumb and forefinger, wrap the thread over the needle.

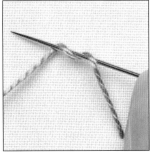

3. Keeping the thread taut, wind it once around the needle in a anti-clockwise direction.

4. Still holding thread taut, turn needle towards the fabric. Place point of the needle onto the fabric at the position for the tip of the stitch.

5. Slide the wraps down onto the fabric. Push the needle through the fabric, maintaining a firm tension on the thread.

6. Pull the thread through keeping your thumb over the knot (thumb not shown). **Completed pistil stitch.**

ASSEMBLING THE BROOCH

The brooch is assembled after the embroidery is completed.

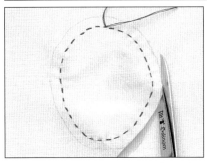

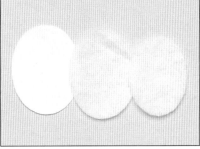

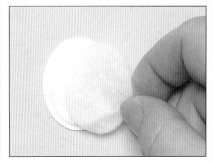

1. Using machine sewing thread, work a row of running stitch 6mm (¹/₄") inside the marked cutting line. Cut out the shape along the cutting line.

2. Cut one piece of wadding to the shape of the card provided with the brooch finding. Cut another piece 2mm (¹/₁₆") smaller than the first.

3. Place the smaller piece of wadding onto the card, then the larger piece.

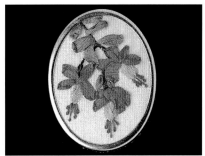

4. Carefully position the embroidered silk over the padded card and draw up the gathering threads. Tie off firmly.

5. Place the embroidery into the brooch. Position the back. With a small coin, press the metal tabs into place.

6. Completed brooch.

PRIVATE COLLECTION

The classic colours of blue-violet, old gold and soft pink have been used in these gracious embroidered pictures created by Susan O'Connor.

Little works of art destined to be loved and admired.

THE POSY

An everlasting bouquet of pink bullion roses, white daisies and blue forget-me-knots is tied with a glorious blue ribbon. A border of white scallops and blue-violet french knots encircles the floral bouquet.

REQUIREMENTS

Fabric
20cm square (8") piece
of white damask

Threads & Needle
Madeira stranded silk
A = white
B = 0812 med shell pink
C = 0813 lt shell pink
D = 0815 ultra lt shell pink
E = 0901 lt blue-violet
F = 1603 lt moss green
G = 2208 lt old gold
No. 12 hand appliqué needle

Supplies
20cm square (8") piece of medium
weight fusible interfacing
15cm (6") embroidery hoop
Sharp lead pencil

EMBROIDERY PREPARATION

See the centre liftout for the embroidery design.

Transferring the design
Trace the design onto paper using a black pen. Tape the tracing to a window or light box. Centre the damask over the tracing and tape in place. The light shining through will make the design visible through the fabric. Using the lead pencil, mark the centres of the flowers and trace the outlines of the bow, stems and scalloped border. Remove the tape from the fabric and tracing.

Preparing the damask
With wrong sides together, iron the interfacing onto the fabric. This gives a more stable surface and makes it easier to maintain an even tension while stitching.

Machine zigzag all edges to prevent the interfacing peeling off.

EMBROIDERY

Bouquet
Place the fabric in the hoop to work the bow only. Embroider the bow first, stitching the loops, ties and finally the bow knot.

Stitch the roses starting each one from its centre and working outwards. The stems and leaves are stitched next. Three pairs of detached chain leaves are evenly spaced around each rose. The stems are long straight stitches couched in place with the same thread.

Embroider the petals of the daisies and forget-me-nots. Add a gold french knot to each one for their centres. Sprinkle pink and white french knots around the edge of the bouquet.

Border
Stitch the two circles of scallops in back stitch. Add tiny blue-violet french knots following the curves of the scallops.

EMBROIDERY KEY

All embroidery is worked using one strand of thread.

Roses
Centre = B (bullion loop, 10 wraps)
Inner petals = C
(3 bullion knots, 10 wraps)
Outer petals = D
(5 bullion knots, 10 wraps)

White daisies
Centre = G (french knot, 2 wraps)
Petals = A (detached chain)

Forget-me-nots
Centre = G (french knot, 2 wraps)
Petals = E (french knot, 2 wraps)

Stems and leaves
Stems = F (straight stitch, couching)
Leaves = F (detached chain)
Scattered knots = A or D
(french knot, 1 wrap)

Bow = E (satin stitch)

Border
Scallops = A (back stitch)
Spots = E (french knot, 1 wrap)

THESE DESIGNS USE:

Straight stitch   Detached chain
Bullion knot   French knot
Back stitch   Satin stitch
Couching   Split Stitch
Long and short stitch

W H E N   T O   U S E   A   H O O P

Hoops are designed to hold the fabric taut while stitching, thus preventing unsightly puckering in your work.

Embroidery stitches fall into two categories - those that are 'skimmed' (eg chain stitch, stem stitch, fly stitch and bullion knots) and those that are 'stabbed' (eg french knot, straight stitch, satin stitch, split stitch and couching).

Skimmed stitches are generally worked in one movement and from one side of the fabric only.

These stitches are best worked without a hoop so the fabric can be manipulated. Stabbed stitches are generally worked in two steps. The needle is taken to the back of the fabric and pulled through before returning it to the front.

While some stitches can be either 'skimmed' or 'stabbed' (eg satin stitch), stabbing produces a better result. A hoop is a valuable aid when working stabbed stitches.

THE BLUEBIRDS

Cascading white ribbon, studded with little sprays of roses, daisies and forget-me-nots, is held in the beaks of two sparkling bluebirds. A heart of french knots complements the background of subtle white damask.

REQUIREMENTS

Fabric

20cm square (8") piece of white damask

Threads & Needle

Madeira stranded silk

A = white
B = 0402 lt terracotta
C = 0812 med shell pink
D = 0813 lt shell pink
E = 0815 ultra lt shell pink
F = 0901 lt blue-violet
G = 1603 lt moss green
H = 2208 lt old gold
No. 12 hand appliqué needle

Supplies

20cm square (8") piece of medium weight fusible interfacing
15cm (6") embroidery hoop
Sharp lead pencil

EMBROIDERY PREPARATION

See the centre liftout for the embroidery design.

Transferring the design

Trace the embroidery design onto paper using a black pen. Tape the tracing to a window or light box. Centre the damask over the tracing and tape in place. The light shining through will make the design visible through the fabric. Using the lead pencil, mark the centres of the flowers and trace the outlines of the bluebirds and ribbons.

Use a tiny dot to mark the positions of the french knots that form the heart and trails. Remove the tape from the fabric and the tracing.

Preparing the damask

With wrong sides together, iron the interfacing onto the fabric. This gives a more stable surface and makes it easier to maintain an even tension while stitching.

Machine zigzag all edges to prevent the interfacing from peeling off.

EMBROIDERY

Place the fabric in the hoop while working the birds and ribbon. Hold the fabric freely in your hand for the remainder of the embroidery.

The bluebirds are embroidered first. Stitch the wings in long and short stitch, then the body, starting from the head and proceeding to the tail. Work a single french knot for the eye and surround it with a detached chain. The beak is satin stitched in two sections.

Next, work the white ribbon in satin stitch. Add the four bullion roses and stitch three pairs of detached chain leaves around each one.

Stitch the petals of the daisies and forget-me-nots. Finish each one with a gold french knot centre.

Embroider the gold trails, beginning with two wrap french knots near the sprays.

The last two knots on each trail are one wrap french knots. Finally, embroider white french knots around the heart, carrying the thread on the back of the fabric between knots.

EMBROIDERY KEY

All embroidery is worked using one strand of thread unless otherwise specified.

Bluebirds

Body = F (split stitch, long and short stitch)
Eye = A (french knot, 2 wraps), B (detached chain)
Beak = H (satin stitch)

Roses

Centre = C (bullion loop, 10 wraps)
Inner petals = D (3 bullion knots, 10 wraps)
Outer petals = E (5 bullion knots, 10 wraps)

White daisies

Centre = H (french knot, 2 wraps)
Petals = A (detached chain)

Forget-me-nots

Centre = H (french knot, 2 wraps)
Petals = F (french knot, 2 wraps)
Leaves = G (detached chain)

Ribbon = A (satin stitch)

Heart = A (french knot, 2 wraps)

Gold trails = H (french knot, 1 - 2 wraps)

HINTS ON RANDOM LONG AND SHORT STITCH

1. Keep the stitches moving in the same direction as the body shape.

In Japanese embroidery this is known as 'stitching with the life force', and it is well worth remembering when stitching any living thing, be it a flower or a bird.

2. When starting a new row, work well into the previous row of stitching and try to split the threads of the previous row with the thread of the new one.

This allows the colours and stitches to merge with one another and eliminates definite lines between the rows of stitching.

3. The bluebirds will look more realistic and 'feathery', if you keep the length of the stitches as random as possible.

STEP-BY-STEP STITCH INSTRUCTIONS NOT INCLUDED IN THIS ARTICLE CAN BE FOUND ON THE FOLLOWING PAGES.

Couching - page 27
Detached chain - page 46
French knot - page 40
Satin stitch - page 9
Split Stitch - page 9
Straight stitch - page 46

BULLION ROSE

A bullion knot is a raised stitch of twisted thread lying on top of the fabric.

Bullion knots are perfect for creating delicate roses on all types of fabric, from the finest voiles to wool.

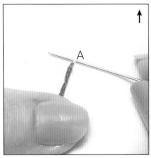

1. Centre. Secure the thread with a back stitch and bring it to the front at A. Take a tiny stitch very close to A. Leave the needle in the fabric.

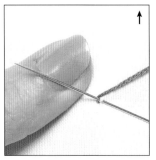

2. Hold your thumb under the needle to keep the needle off the fabric. Take the thread under the needle.

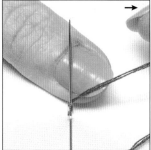

3. Rotate the fabric so the needle faces upwards and away from you. Wrap the thread clockwise once around the needle.

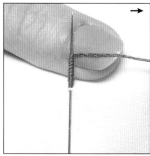

4. Wrap the thread evenly around the needle nine more times. Use your thumb and forefinger to keep the wraps on the needle. Ensure the wraps sit close together.

5. Placing your left thumb on the wraps to hold them firmly, begin to ease the eye of the needle through the wraps.

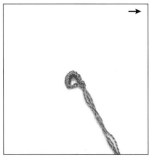

6. Keeping your thumb on the wraps, continue pulling until the two ends of the loop come together and the wraps are tight.

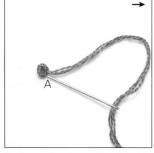

7. Press the loop firmly with your thumb so it lies flat on the fabric. Take the needle to the back at A. End off on the back of the fabric with a tiny back stitch.

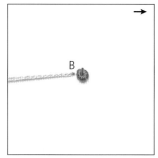

8. Inner petals. Rotate the fabric. Change to a lighter shade and secure the thread on the back. Bring needle to front at B, halfway along one side of loop.

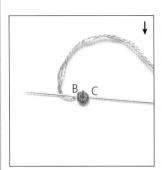

9. Take the needle from C to B, leaving it in the fabric. Each inner petal will form a half circle.

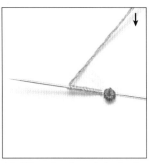

10. Wrap the thread clock-wise around the needle ten times.

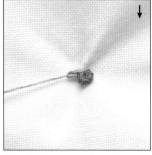

11. With your thumb over the wraps, pull the needle and thread tightly until the fabric forms a pleat. (Thumb not shown.)

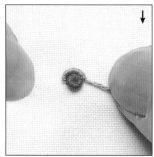

12. Stretch the fabric flat again. This will cause the stitch to fall into position.

Ensure the wraps sit close together at the base of the needle. Loose wraps will cause large loops to form when the stitch is pulled through.

Use a straw (milliner's) needle as it is easier to pull through than other needles and does not distort the wraps as it passes through them.

If if it is difficult to pull the needle through, slightly twist the needle in the opposite direction to the direction of the wraps. This will loosen the wraps and allow the needle to be pulled through.

With bullion knots you will often get one stubborn little loop that won't pull through. Get tough - most embroidery threads are extremely strong. Hold the knot on the fabric with your thumb and pull hard until the offending loop disappears.

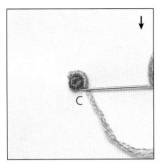

13. Take the needle to the back at C.

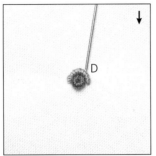

14. Pull the thread through. Re-emerge at D.

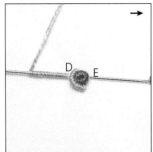

15. Rotate the fabric. Take the needle from E to D. Wrap the thread around the needle ten times.

16. Pull the thread through. Take the needle to the back at E to complete the second petal. Bring the thread to the front at F.

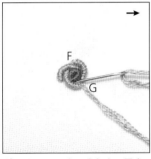

17. Rotate the fabric. Take the needle from G (between the centre and first petal) to F. Wrap ten times. Take the needle to the back at G.

18. Pull the thread through and end off. Outer petals. Change to a lighter shade. Bring the thread to the front at H.

19. Rotate the fabric. Take the needle from I to H and wrap the thread ten times. Complete the bullion knot as before.

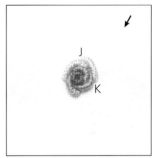

20. Bring the needle to the front at J. Rotate the fabric. Work a ten wrap bullion knot from K to J.

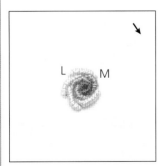

21. Bring the needle to the front at L. Rotate the fabric. Work a ten wrap bullion knot from M to L.

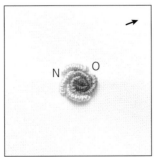

22. Bring the needle to the front at N. Rotate the fabric. Work a ten wrap bullion knot from O to N.

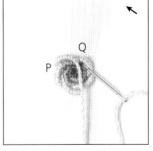

23. Bring the needle to the front at P. Rotate the fabric. Work a ten wrap bullion knot from Q to P. Q is just inside the first bullion knot of this round.

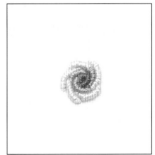

24. Pull the thread through and end off on the back of the fabric.
Completed bullion rose.

BACK STITCH

Back stitch is particularly suited to fine lines and details. It is often used to form the foundation of several other stitches.

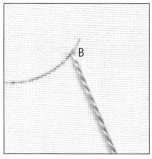 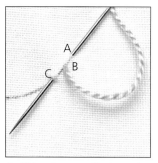 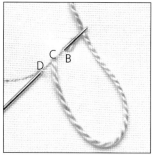 

1. Bring the thread to the front at B, approximately 1.5mm ($^1/_{16}$") from the start of the marked design.

2. Take the needle into the fabric at the starting point (A). Re-emerge 1.5mm ($^1/_{16}$") beyond B at C.

3. Pull thread through to complete first stitch. Take needle to back at B in exactly the same hole. Re-emerge at D, 3mm ($^1/_8$") away.

4. Continue working stitches in the same manner. To end off, take the thread through the hole at the beginning of the previous stitch.

LONG AND SHORT STITCH

In conventional long and short stitch, only the stitches of the first row vary in length. Here, the length of all the straight stitches varies and the stitches in one row may split the stitches of the previous row. We used three shades of thread for photographic purposes only.

1. Place the fabric in a hoop. Outline the shape to be filled using split stitch. This helps create a neat edge.

2. First row of stitches. Bring the thread to the front just beyond the stitched outline.

3. Take it to the back within the shape. Work a row of straight stitches alternating a longer stitch with a shorter stitch. Angle the stitches slightly, following the shape.

4. Second row of stitches. Bring the needle to the front at A. Take it to the back close to the first stitch of the first row (splitting the stitch if necessary).

5. Bring the needle to the front at B. Take it to the back close to a stitch in the first row.

6. Continue working across the row, varying the length of the stitches and staggering their starting positions.

7. While stitches are kept as parallel as possible to each other, stitches may need to be angled slightly to suit the shape. Do this as gradually and gently as possible.

8. Continue until the entire shape is filled and the outline is completely hidden. **Completed long and short stitch.**

LACING THE EMBROIDERY

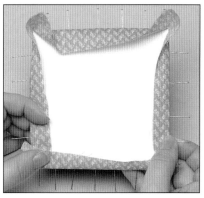

Before being placed in its frame, the embroidery needs to be laced over a piece of card to hold the surface flat and free from wrinkles.

Never glue, staple or tape needlework, as the chemicals and metal used in these processes will lead to the deterioration of the fabric and threads over the passage of time.

Most good framers provide a lacing service but it will save on the cost of framing if you do it yourself. Ask your framer for a suitable piece of card.

It may improve the appearance of some embroideries if there is a layer of thin wadding placed between the card and the fabric to pad the surface slightly.

1. Cut a piece of stiff card at least 1cm (³/₈") larger on all sides than the hole in the framing mount. Position the card over the wrong side of the embroidered fabric. Fold excess fabric over. Starting at the middle and working out to the corners, pin into the ends of the card. Do one side, then the opposite side. Pin the remaining sides in the same manner.

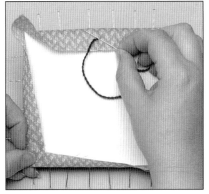

2. Cut a long length of woollen yarn and thread through a sharp-pointed needle. On the back of the card, and beginning in the centre of one side, secure the yarn to the overlapping fabric.

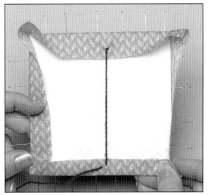

3. Take a 6mm (¹/₄") stitch into all layers of overlapping fabric on the opposite side of the card. This stitch reduces the stress to any one spot in the fabric.

4. Pull yarn firmly and hold to retain the tension. Take a 6mm (¹/₄") stitch on the opposite side, close to the first stitch. Again, pull the yarn firmly.

5. Checking to ensure the front is smooth and free from wrinkles, continue working from side to side until you reach the end of the card. Tighten the lacing and end off securely.

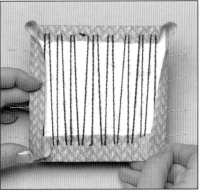

6. Join in the yarn at the centre again and repeat the procedure to the other side of the card.

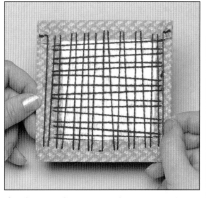

7. Secure the yarn at the centre of one unworked side. Repeat steps 3 - 6 for the remaining sides, ensuring the front is smooth and free from wrinkles.
Completed lacing.

designed by **Wendy Dimmick of Victoria**

GAY ABANDON

DAZZLING COTTON TEA TOWELS

THE SUNFLOWER APRON

The colourful apron is made from cotton tea towels.
An appliquéd sunflower is embellished with carefully
chosen stitches including blanket stitch, twisted
chain and whipped chain stitch.
A little piece of wearable art to add gaiety to your soul.

REQUIREMENTS FOR SUNFLOWER APRON

Fabric
72cm x 52cm wide
(28 ³/8" x 20 ¹/2") brightly
coloured cotton tea towel
12cm square (4 ³/4") piece of
royal blue cotton headcloth
17cm x 15cm wide
(6 ³/4" x 6") piece of dark
green cotton headcloth
15cm square (6") piece of
bright yellow cotton
headcloth
5cm square (2") piece of
ochre cotton headcloth

Threads & Needle
DMC stranded cotton
A = 350 med coral
B = 367 dk pistachio green
C = 740 tangerine
D = 742 lt tangerine
E = 783 med topaz
F = 796 dk royal blue
No. 8 crewel needle

Supplies
17cm x 40cm wide
(6 ³/4" x 15 ³/4") piece of
appliqué paper or double-
sided fusible webbing
1.8m x 12mm wide (2yd x ¹/2")
natural cotton webbing
Sharp lead pencil
Chalk-based fabric marker

EMBROIDERY PREPARATION
See the centre liftout for the embroidery design. See page 78 for step-by-step instructions for fusing appliqué paper.

Marking design placements
Fold the tea towel in half length-wise. From the top edge, measure down 19.5cm (7³/4") along the fold.

Mark the position with the fabric marker. This is the centre of the sunflower. Again from the top edge, measure down 48.5cm (19") along the fold and mark this position *(diag 1)*.

This is the position for the base of the pot.

Diag 1

Transferring the design
Trace the entire design onto tracing paper.

Pin the tracing to the right side of the tea towel, matching the placement marks with the corresponding parts of the design.

Using a large needle, pierce holes in the tracing along all outlines. Dot each hole with the fabric marker and remove the tracing.

Preparing the appliqué pieces
Using the lead pencil, trace the required shapes onto the appliqué paper. Cut each one out just beyond the design lines. Iron the appliqué paper pieces onto the wrong sides of the appropriate fabric. Carefully cut out each shape exactly. Peel away the backing paper and position the stem and leaves on the tea towel.

Carefully press to fuse the fabric to the tea towel. Repeat this procedure for the pot, the petals and then the centre of the sunflower.

EMBROIDERY
Starting at a corner, outline the entire pot in blanket stitch. The rim of the pot is one line of couching. Work two rows of chain stitch along the stem keeping the adjacent stitches even in length. Starting at the top, whip the outer half of the right hand row. When reaching the base, turn the fabric upside down and whip the outer half of the remaining row.

The adjacent inner halves are then whipped together. Starting from the stem, outline the leaves in a single row of chain stitch.

The entire circle of ochre fabric is covered with lattice couching. Use the topaz thread for the long laid stitches and the coral thread for the tiny crosses that couch the laid threads in place.

Stitch a circle of chain stitch around the edge of the ochre fabric. Approximately 6mm (¹/₄") out from this circle, work a second circle in twisted chain stitch. Fill the space between the two circles with scattered french knots.

To work each petal, start from the circle and stem stitch to the edge of the yellow fabric. Change to blanket stitch and embroider the outer section of the petal. Continue stitching the petals in this manner, completing one before starting the next.

CONSTRUCTION

Place the embroidered tea towel face down on a flat surface. From one top corner, measure 14cm (5 ¹/₂") across the top edge. Mark the position with the fabric marker. Beginning at the same corner, measure down 25.5cm (10") along the side and mark.

With wrong sides together, fold the tea towel at the marks. Press and pin in place. Repeat the procedure for the remaining corner. Machine stitch around the edge of each of the folded corners *(diag 2)*.

Diag 2

Cut two pieces of cotton webbing, each 58cm long (23") for the ties and one piece 64cm long (25 ¹/₄") for the neck. Neaten both ends of each piece by folding under 6mm (¹/₄") twice and stitching along the fold.

Machine stitch one tie to each side just below the previously folded corner. Stitch each end of the longer piece of tape to either end of the top edge.

EMBROIDERY KEY

All embroidery is worked with four strands of thread.

Flower
Inner centre = A and E (lattice couching), A (chain stitch)
Outer centre = C (twisted chain stitch, french knot, 1 wrap)
Petals = D (stem stitch, blanket stitch)

Leaves and stem
Leaves = B (chain stitch)
Stem = B (whipped chain stitch)

Pot
Outline = F (blanket stitch)
Rim = F (couching)

THE TULIP APRON

Transforming function into fun, the dramatic tulip apron is made in the same manner as the sunflower apron. Ideal as a coverup in the kitchen or garden, they are both easy to assemble and embroider.

REQUIREMENTS FOR TULIP APRON

Fabric
66cm x 47cm wide (26" x 18 1/2") bright coloured cotton tea towel
7cm x 14cm wide (2 3/4" x 5 1/2") piece of hot pink cotton headcloth
9cm x 10cm wide (3 1/2" x 4") piece of royal blue cotton headcloth
6cm square (2 3/8") piece of jade cotton headcloth

Threads & Needle
DMC stranded cotton
A = 601 dk cranberry
B = 791 vy dk cornflower blue
C = 958 dk seagreen
No. 8 crewel needle

Supplies
9cm x 25cm wide (3 1/2" x 9 3/4") piece of appliqué paper or double-sided fusible webbing
1.8m x 12mm wide (2yd x 1/2") natural cotton webbing
Sharp lead pencil
Chalk-based fabric marker

EMBROIDERY PREPARATION
See the centre liftout for the embroidery design.

Marking design placements
Fold the tea towel in half lengthwise. From the top edge, measure down 14.5cm (5 3/4") along the fold.

Mark the position with the fabric marker.

This is the position of the right hand petal of the larger tulip. Again from the top, measure down 34cm (13 3/8") along the fold and mark this position *(diag 1)*. This is the position for the base of the pot.

Diag 1

Transferring the design
Transfer the design to the tea towel and prepare the pieces of fabric for appliquéing in the same manner as for the Sunflower apron.

EMBROIDERY
Starting at one corner, outline the pot with two rows of chain stitch. Work the inner row on the edge of the appliquéd fabric then the outer row next to it on the tea towel. A single line of couching marks the rim of the pot.

Embroider the stems with two rows of chain stitch directly onto the tea towel. Outline the leaves in blanket stitch starting each one at the stem and working the stitches close together.

The upper leaf has a couched centre vein.

The petals of both flowers are outlined with twisted chain stitch.

EMBROIDERY KEY
All embroidery is worked with four strands of thread.

Flower
Petal outlines = A (twisted chain stitch)

Leaves and stem
Leaf outlines = C (blanket stitch)
Leaf vein = C (couching)
Stem = C (whipped chain stitch)

Pot
Outline = B (chain stitch)
Rim = B (couching)

CONSTRUCTION
Assemble the apron following the instructions for the sunflower apron.

STEP-BY-STEP STITCH INSTRUCTIONS NOT INCLUDED IN THIS ARTICLE CAN BE FOUND ON THE FOLLOWING PAGES.

Couching - page 27
French knot - page 40
Stem stitch - page 46

FUSING APPLIQUÉ PAPER

This technique ensures the fabric shapes will not move out of position when you stitch them to the fabric.

  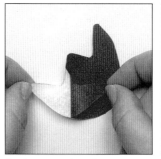 

1. Trace the design onto the wrong side of the appliqué paper and cut out just outside the design lines.

2. Place right side of paper onto the wrong side of the fabric. Press. Lift the iron to move from one place to the next rather than pushing it.

3. Cut out the shape to its exact size. Carefully peel off the backing paper.

4. Place the motif right side up onto the right side of the fabric. Fuse in place using a press-and-lift motion until the shape is firmly attached.

BLANKET STITCH

Blanket stitch is used to appliqué the fabric to the tea towels. It gives a finished edge to the cut fabric.

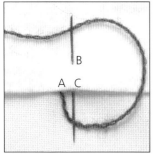 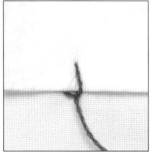 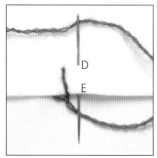 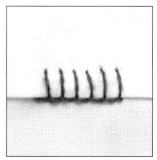

1. Bring the thread to the front at A, through the base fabric only. Take the needle through both layers at B and re-emerge at C through the base fabric only.

2. With the thread under the tip of the needle, pull it through until the stitch sits snugly against the cut edge of the fabric but does not distort it.

3. Take the needle to the back at D through both layers. Re-emerge at E, next to the cut edge of the appliqué fabric.

4. Continue working evenly spaced stitches. To end off, take the needle to the back at the edge just over the last stitch. **Completed blanket stitch.**

LATTICE COUCHING

The foundation of this composite stitch is made from a grid of long diagonal straight stitches which are couched at the intersections with small cross stitches.

   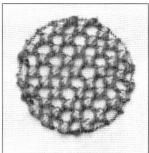

1. Work long diagonal straight stitches across the entire area to be filled. Space the stitches approximately 5mm (³/16") apart.
Work a second set of diagonal straight stitches in the opposite direction.

2. Couching. Change thread. Bring it to the front just below the first intersection of two straight stitches on the left hand side. Take the thread to the back just above the intersection.

3. Re-emerge just to the left of the intersection. Take the thread to the back on the right hand side of the intersection forming a small cross.

4. Re-emerge just below the second intersection. Continue working crosses in the same manner along the laid stitches until all the intersections are couched in place. **Completed lattice couching.**

CHAIN STITCH

Take care not to pull the loops too tight as this distorts the fabric and the stitches lose their rounded appearance.

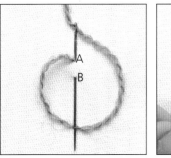

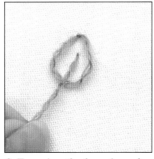

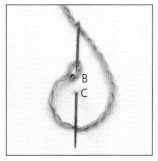

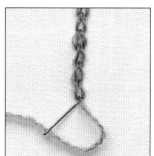

1. Bring the thread to the front at A. Take the needle to the back through the same hole. The thread forms a loop. Re-emerge at B.

2. Ensuring the loop is under the tip of the needle, begin to pull the thread through.

3. Continue pulling until loop tightens around thread. Take needle from B to C to begin the second stitch and to complete the first stitch.

4. Continue stitching in the same manner. To secure the last stitch, take the needle to the back just over the loop.

TWISTED CHAIN STITCH

Twisted chain stitch is a variation of normal chain stitch. The added twist gives the stitch a rope-like effect.

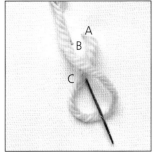

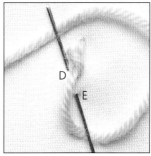

1. Bring needle to front at A. Take needle to the back at B and re-emerge at C. The loop is under the needle and the needle is angled slightly towards the centre.

2. Gently pull the thread through to form the first twisted chain stitch.

3. Take the needle from D to E to anchor the first stitch and to begin the second stitch. The thread forms an anti-clockwise loop under the needle.

4. Continue working stitches in the same manner. To end off, take the needle to the back just over the last loop.

WHIPPED CHAIN STITCH

Whipped chain is worked over a foundation of chain stitch. The whipping wraps the chain stitches and does not go through the fabric.

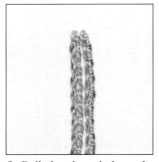

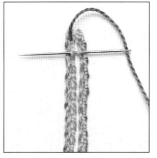

1. Work two rows of adjacent chain stitch to form the foundation. With a new thread, bring needle to front in centre of the first right hand stitch. Take needle through next stitch below. Do not go through fabric.

2. Pull the thread through. Take the needle through the third loop from right to left. Continue in this manner to the end. Work the remaining outer edge in the same way.

3. To whip two rows together as for the centre of the sunflower and tulip stems, take the needle through the loop on the right hand side and re-emerge in the loop on the left. Again, do not go through the fabric.

4. Continue along centre stitches in the same manner to complete the row of whipped chain stitch.

*Special thanks to
our contributors who made
this book possible*

Kris Richards

Denise Bakes

Sharon Paton

Annie Humphris

Jennifer Newman

Phil Drew

Maree Moscato

Carolyn Pearce

Liz Kulinski

Marjorie Kavanagh

Wendy Dimmick